John McNeil

So You Want to Write a Java Desktop Application

A Trivial File Transfer Protocol Client

Software Pulse

2019

Software Pulse,
www.softwarepulse.co.uk

ISBN: 978-0-224-75412-9

So You Want to Build a Java Desktop Application!

A Trivial File Transfer Protocol Client

This book takes you step by step through the process of building a Java application. We start with a basic description of the application and examine exactly how each part works.

Having gained an understanding of how the application should function the various components are broken out. We look at how the user will need to interact with the application and how we can make an easy to use experience. We look at the various components of the solution, breaking down the problem into logical parts. This approach makes it easier to solve the overall problem as well as reducing errors caused by large complex items of code.

Once the application design is complete, we start to build the solution via the logical components identified in our design. As each section of code is added we explain what we are doing and why and how this works with the rest of the code. Even if your understanding of Java is fairly basic the explanations are designed to allow you to understand the intention and therefore help you decompose the code.

At the end of the book you get to test your application and prove your solution. The material covered here will allow you to take the techniques here to design and build you own applications.

Happy coding!

Contents

Introduction

Welcome to "So you want to build a Java desktop application" a tutorial on JavaFX. The idea behind this material is to show how to build a real application in JavaFX. A real solution not a series of examples of what you can do but something that can be used, something that serves a purpose.

The actual application is based on a specification document by the Network Working Group: Request for Change (RFC) 1350 https://www.ietf.org/wg/. This specification describes how to implement what is known as a Trivial File Transfer Protocol (TFTP). This is described as a simplified version of the File Transfer Protocol specification so is ideal to use as an example. There are two parts to this, a client and a server so, for our JavaFX application we will build a TFTP client. There are also TFTP servers freely available, so we have a server that we can test our client against.

To build our application we will use Eclipse with Java SE version 8. To help build the JavaFX user interface we will use Gluon Scene Builder. See the appendix for how to download and install the tools we will use in building this application.

All the code for the application is presented here so that you can type it in as you go. There are advantages in taking the time to type in the code, it allows your mind the opportunity to digest each line and improves understanding of the text. If typing in all the code presented does here seems a little daunting to you then we have an alternative. The complete source code for the application can be found on the website http://softwarepulse.co.uk.

Trivial File Transfer

Let's look at the RFC1350 specification so that we understand what TFTP is and what we need to do to build a client application.

TFTP is described in the specification as a simple protocol to transfer files and hence it was named Trivial File Transfer Protocol (TFTP). Importantly it is built on top of Internet User Datagram Protocol (UDP) and this is different from how traditional File Transfer Protocol (FTP) works but also makes for a simpler implementation.

Like FTP, TFTP is designed to move files from one system to another, so files can be copied to a server or copied from a server. As TFTP is designed to be a small lightweight application it does lack the features found in the full FTP solution but that also means that it focuses on the transfer part without all the none core features. So, all you can expect from TFTP is the ability to move files between systems.

The TFTP RFC specifies three modes of transfer, octet, netascii and mail. Although mail is mentioned in the RFC it is obsolete and should not be implemented or used so, that leaves us two modes of transfer. The netascii mode is for transferring text-based files between systems. This is useful when you want to move a text file between Windows, Linux and Macintosh machines. Each of these machines may use a different line terminator so if you simply copy the file from one machine to another then it would not display correctly. By transferring the file using netascii, the line terminators are replaced with that defined in the RFC document for transfer and then converted to the native line terminator of the target machine when it arrives thus ensuring the file displays correctly when opened on the target machine.

The other method is using octet, some people may be familiar with the term 'binary transfer' which is used to move the actual bytes of a file from one location to another on the same host and thus not altering the file contents. With TFTP octet is used as it removes the ambiguity that can be found when moving across systems where storage sizes may differ.

So that covers the types of transfer TFTP supports.

Transfer mechanism

To transfer a file using TFTP there needs to be a TFTP server waiting to receive requests and a TFTP client to initiate a transfer. The server listens for connection requests from any clients. Once a request is received the server processes the request and responds. The client in turn, responds to the server's message and the client and server continue their exchange of messages until the request is complete.

The client can initiate one of two types of request, a request to send a file to the server 'Write' or a request to receive a file from the server 'Read'.

When requesting a file from the server 'Read' the client sends to the server the name of the file it is looking for. Providing the server can locate the requested file the server will send back a packet of data containing the first part of the file or, the entire file if it fits within the packet size.

There is no concept of directories specified in the TFTP RFC, all files are assumed to be in the server or clients defined file repository.

Along with the first part of the file the server will send a packet counter starting at 1 (one). Each subsequent packet of data will increment the counter by 1. The client on the receiving end can then use the packet counter to ensure it receives all the packets of data. As can be seen from this, the TFTP specification ensures that packets of data are transmitted sequentially and in order. This makes the implementation simple and light weight and ideal for firmware implementations.

Each packet of data makes provision for 512 bytes of data. As long as the client receives a packet with 512 bytes of data it knows that the transmission is still ongoing. When a packet of less than 512 bytes of data is received then this is the final packet of data and no more packets are expected from the server.

For each packet of data the client receives from the server, it sends an acknowledgement back to the server containing the last packet counter received. On receipt of the acknowledgement the server can then send the next packet of data otherwise it resends the last packet of data assuming the previous attempt was lost.

If the client request is to send a file to the server then a Write request is sent to the server and the server responds as it would for a 'Read' request but the packet sequence number the server sends is 0 (zero) and then the client responds with packet number 1 (one) and the conversation starts from there.

Establishing communication

TFTP servers listen for connections on port 69. Any TFTP client that wishes to initiate a request must send the initial UPD request to the server on port 69. As part of the UPD request the client will specify the port number that the client will use to listen for a response and therefore the port the server should address its response to. The port ranges are specified as being in the range of 0 (zero) to 65,535, although it would be prudent to avoid the commonly used ports and keep to the high-end numbers.

The server will send any response to the client IP number and port used in the UDP message and will now allocate a port which the server will listen on for the remainder of the conversation. In this way, port 69 can be kept free for other connection requests.

The client should then send all other responses to the server on the new port until the conversation completes.

Data Transfer Mechanics

To initiate a transfer the client must send a request as a UDP packet. The data wrapped in the UDP packet contains information on the type of transfer request, Read or Write, the name of the file, and the transfer mode to use either "Octet" or "Netascii".

In response, the server will send one of three types of response, data (DATA), acknowledgement (ACK) or error (ERR). If the request is a Read then the server will send data packets and the client will send acknowledgement packets. If the request is to Write a file on the server then the server sends acknowledgements and the client sends data packets. Error packets are used when an error condition is met, although TFTP only has a few error conditions such as file not found.

The operation codes supported in TFTP are:

01.   Read request (RRQ)

02.   Write request (WRQ)

03.   Data (DATA)

04.   Acknowledgment (ACK)

05.   Error (ERROR)

The structure of the Read/Write request packet is as follows: -

```
2 bytes     string    1 byte      string    1 byte
-----------------------------------------------------
| Opcode |  Filename  |   0   |     Mode    |   0   |
-----------------------------------------------------
```

If the request is a Write the server will respond with an Acknowledgement with a block number of zero '0' otherwise it would use the block number received in the data packet. The packet would be constructed according to the structure below:

```
        2 bytes      2 bytes
        ----------------------
        | Opcode |   Block #  |
        ----------------------
```

The client would, upon receipt of the ACK from the server, send a Data packet containing up to 512 bytes of data and increment the block number by 1 in the following structure:

```
        2 bytes      2 bytes        n bytes
        ----------------------------------------
        | Opcode |   Block #  |    Data      |
        ----------------------------------------
```

The exchange between client and server would continue until a data packet is received which contains less than 512 bytes of data signalling the end of the file transfer.

If a packet gets lost in transit, then each party will resend their last message. So, for the sender, if they do not receive an ACK after a period of time then they will resend the data packet to the other party. If the receiver has sent an ACK and is expecting a data packet but does not receive it then the ACK is resent. Each party will determine how many resends they will send before they give up and the connection is terminated.

In the event an error should occur then the error structure can be used to notify the other party. An error message would look like this:

```
   2 bytes       2 bytes         string      1 byte

   ------------------------------------------------

  | Opcode |   ErrorCode |    ErrMsg    |   0   |

   ------------------------------------------------
```

The error codes supported by TFTP are as follows:

Value   Meaning

Value	Meaning
0	Not defined, see error message (if any).
1	File not found.
2	Access violation
3	Disk full or allocation exceeded.
4	Illegal TFTP operation.
5	Unknown transfer ID.
6	File already exists.
7	No such user.

The User Interface

Now we have an understanding of how TFTP works and what our client needs to do let's turn our attention to the client application. First off, we make a stab at the information our client will need to handle. For instance the application will need to be able to make a call to a server. It will also need to specify if the request is to read or write. Then the name of the file will need to be provided. We could specify the client port to use or we could dynamically allocate one. Then we need a means to report back to the user what is happening; what if the server can't find the file requested.

So, with all that in mind we could have an interface something like this:

Figure 1 sketch of the user interface

The interface will make use of text fields, drop down lists, buttons, labels and a text area. To capture the server ip number will use a simple text field. The direction which we are using to indicate if we want to read or write a file will use of a drop-down list. The list will offer one of two options, either PUT for writing a file or GET for reading a file. Then we have the Mode, this is also a drop-down list containing two options from which the user will select one. This is used to indicate if the file transfer should be a binary or netascii transfer. The last of the input fields is the Filename and as it suggests this is the name of the file that we want to transfer.

Below these fields we have two buttons, the Go button used to send the data from the fields above to the TFTP server. The Clear button allows the user to clear all the field values so that they can perform another action

The last field is the Status field and this, as it might suggest, provides the user with feedback on the progress of their request as well as confirmation that the request is complete.

So that's our user interface, simple and clean.

Structuring the Application

Turning our attention to the code, how are we going to put this together? Well, as with all JavaFX applications we will need to create a class extended from JavaFX Application. Let's call ours TftpClient.

Our application entry point will be responsible for loading our user interface. Before we get into talking about the loading of the UI lets first take a look at how JavaFX is structured.

When introducing JavaFX it is usual to talk about the stage, the scene and the items within the scene. Due to the terms used, it is often likened to a Theatre: the stage is the main display platform or in our case the application window. The scenes can be added to the stage and changed as required and then various items can be laid within the scenes.

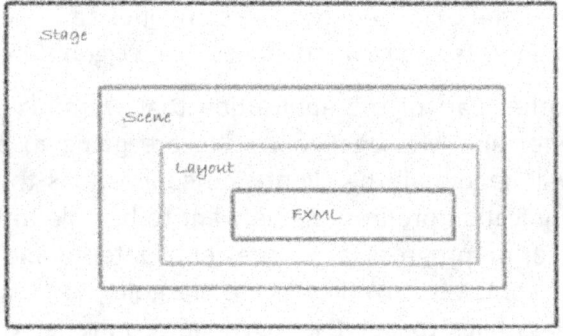

Figure 2 JavaFX presentation layers

So back to our application entry point. This class takes care of loading our stage, into which goes our scene and then we add the layout to which we have loaded our FXML file containing information about the items for our scene.

The FMXL file has within it a statement of the class that should be used as a controller. The controller is used to set up the initial values of the items defined in the file as well as handling events triggered by the UI items.

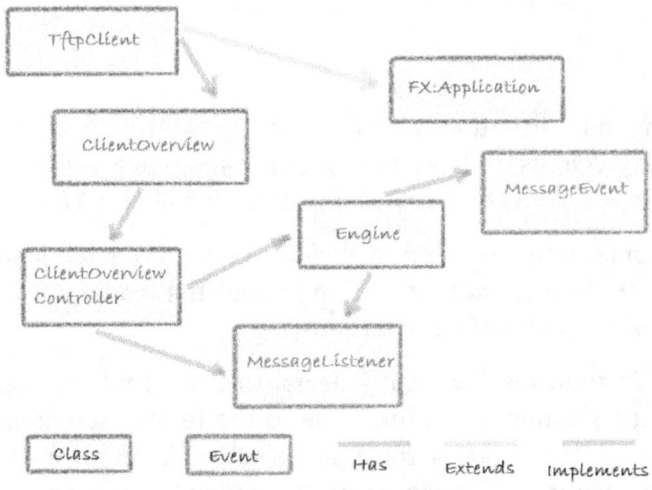

Figure 3 class structure for application

So now when the UI is rendered, we can populate our fields with default values, set up our lists and react to any events triggered by our front end.

The only other part of the application that warrants a mention is the MessageListener and MessageEvent. We are going to create an Engine class which will handle all the client-side connections to the TFTP server. As the communication progresses, we want to be able to feed information back to the user on progress, any issues encountered and notification that the transfer is complete. To do this we are going to MessageEvents from our Engine class back to our ClientOverviewController which in turn will update our user interface.

So now we have outlined the bare bones of what we are doing let's make a start building code.

Creating the project

Power up Eclipse, with e(fx)clipse installed, and create a new JavaFX Project.

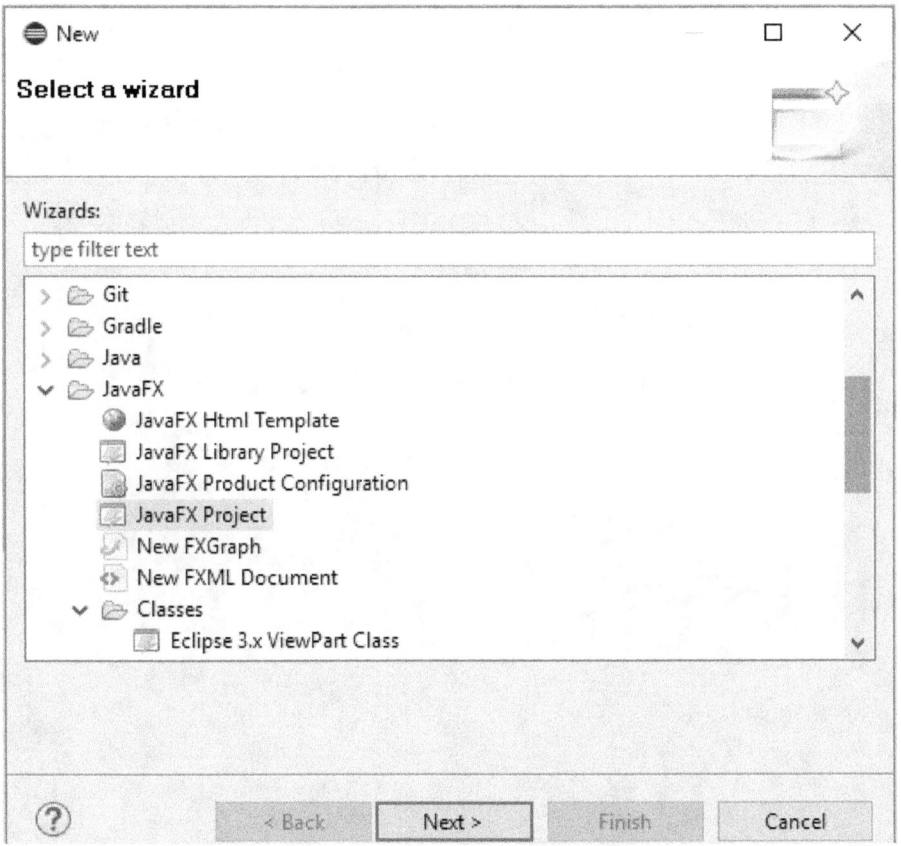

Figure 4 creating new JavaFX project

Give your project a name, for this tutorial I will use TFTPClientDemo. Ensure you are using Java 1.8 for the project otherwise all the defaults can be kept.

By default, this will create a 'src' folder with an 'application' sub folder and two files under the sub folder called 'Main.java' and 'application.css'. For this tutorial, we will delete the files and the application sub folder so we are just left with the 'src' folder.

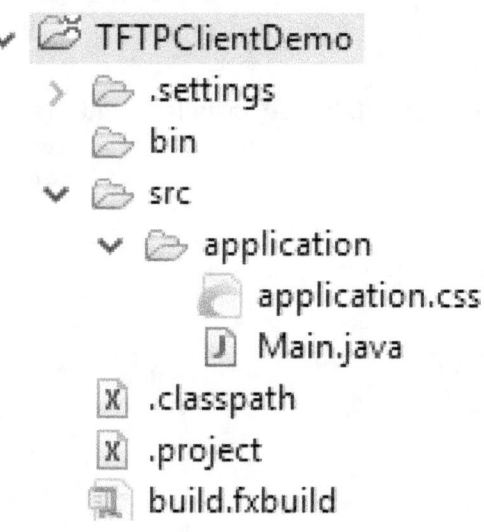

Figure 5 initial JavaFX project structure

The Client UI

There are two methods for creating a UI in JavaFX, one is to use java code and the other is to use the mark-up language, eXtensible Mark-up Language (XML). For this tutorial, we will only be using the XML approach. However, we are only using this approach because we will make use of the Scene Builder tool and this generates the XML for us. We will come back to this in a minute, first let's remind ourselves of what our UI looks like and what actions it needs to support.

Earlier we mocked up what we thought we would need to do for our user interface and it was this:

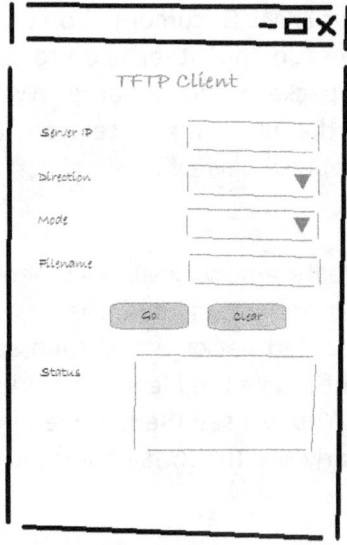

So, looking at our mock-up we will need a label at the top and five labels down the left-hand side.

There will need to be a text field followed by two drop down fields and then another text field.

Next come two buttons the 'Go' and the 'Cancel' buttons, followed finally by a text area field.

The two drop down fields will need to be populated with options and we can make them default to an initial value.

The buttons will need to be linked to actions so when clicked the application will do something. That means we will need to associate the FXML file with a controller.

So now we have a good idea of what we are trying to build we can now create our XML template (FXML Document) for our UI using Scene Builder.

Change to the Eclipse Package workspace explorer otherwise the Scene Builder options will not be available later on when we come to use them.

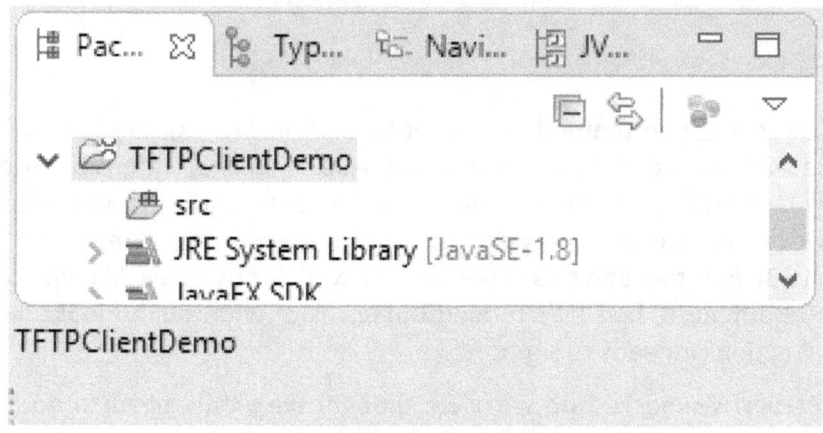

Figure 6 package view of project

First, we will create a package to hold our FXML Document. You are not able to do this as part of the creation process so you either need to create the package first or move it to an existing package once created. We will create the package first. Right click on the project and select 'New – Package'. We will call the package 'softwarepulse.fx.view'.

So, with our package created we will create a new FXML document for our project. To do this, ensure you have the project selected, the best way to do this is to right click on our newly created package and then select 'New – Other – JavaFX/New FXML Document'. Give the file a name, we will use 'ConnectionOverview' and click Finish. You will see the file open in the file viewer pane and from that you will clearly see the XML generated as a stub for the file. We will now build on this.

Close the file in the viewer, this is only to prevent us accidentally modifying the file in two places at the same time and corrupting the file. From the package explorer view, right click on the FXML Document we just created and select 'Open with Scene Builder'. This presents us with a blank document which we will now start to add our objects.

Let us start with a quick tour of the Scene Builder layout so we know what is where.

Figure 7 Scene Builder application

Down the left-hand side are listed, at the top all the objects that we can select to add to our user interface and at the bottom, under the 'Document' section, all the objects we currently have added. The very bottom section labelled 'Controller' is where we will specify what class is to be used as the controller for our scene. We will come back to the controller later.

Now you will notice that currently under the 'Document' section we only show the 'Anchor Pane'. This is a type of pane which determines how objects placed on the pane are aligned. It is similar to a layout region if you have experience of SWING. There other options that can be selected from the Containers section such as border and flow layouts. For this tutorial we will stick with the Anchor Pane.

One the right-hand side are the attributes for the currently selected object. These are split into properties, layout and code. We will explore these as we go through the tutorial.

The centre section is where we lay out the user interface.

So, let's start building our user interface. First, we will set the size of the pane. For this application, we are going to use a fixed size pane with a width of 239 and a height of 342. I must confess that I just made these values up based on the items I wanted to place on the pane. Feel free to alter this to what you think suits, especially if you are building you application in another language where your labels may require different spacing.

To set the pane size, expand the Document section on the left-hand side and select the AnchorPane. On the right-hand side expand the Layout section and locate the 'Pref Width' and 'Pref Height' under the Size section. Change these values to 239 for the width and 342 for the height. This will give you a small rectangular white area within the centre of the scene builder application. This is our scene for adding items.

Next, we will add in our title label to the top of our scene. Expand the controls section and scroll down to locate the "Label" and drag this onto the pane near the top and in the centre. Scene builder will indicate the axis' such as centre of the pane to help with the layout. With the label positioned where you want it, expand the Properties section on the right-hand side and change the value in the Text field to 'TFPT Client' or any value you wish to use. Set the Font to a suitable size and type face. I used 'System' with 14-point size and set the text to bold. You may need to re-centre now the text is longer.

To help line up the labels and fields on the pane we will use a GridPane so, go to the Containers section and drag the GridPane onto the AnchorPane. By default, the GridPane provides 3 rows and 2 columns. We need to add one more row to the GridPane and to do this we can right click on the GridPane object listed in the Document Hierarchy displayed on the left-hand side and then select 'GridPane-Add Row Below'. This now gives us 4 rows. Position the GridPane just below the title label, we will use this to hold the first 4 fields and labels.

Next add 5 other labels, one for each of the fields we will add later. Position the first 4 in the left-hand column of the GridPane. The last one, just place near the bottom of the scene for now. Change the text to reflect the labels of the fields. In my case I have used 'Server IP', 'Direction', 'Mode', 'Filename' and 'Status'.

Next, we will add the fields. From the Controls section select "TextField" and drag it on to the pane and position it to the right of the top label, the one labelled 'Server IP' if you are following my naming. Drag another field over and line this one up with the Filename label.

You will notice that the "TextArea" control is listed just above the "TextField" so drag that over to the pane and line it up with the Status label that we positioned towards the bottom of the scene.

The last 2 fields are the choice boxes so scroll though the Controls to find the "ChoiceBox" field and drag two of these onto the pane to line up with the labels Direction and Mode.

We now have something that looks like this:

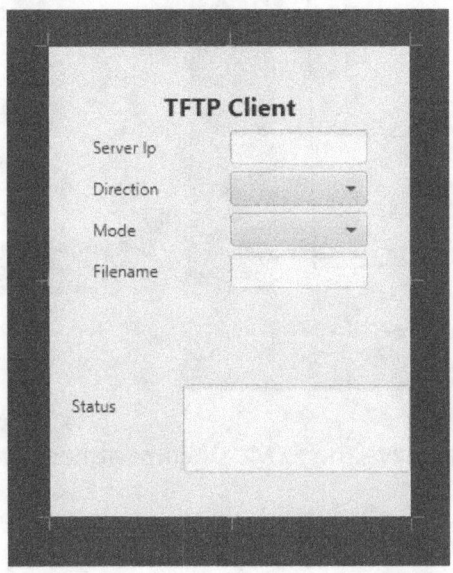

Figure 8 TFTP Client user interface in Scene Builder

What is missing are the buttons and to get these on we will first add a ButtonBar from the Container section and place this just below the GridPane. This gives us a single button by default. We now need to go to the Controls section and add another button. To rename our buttons so they describe the function they perform we select a button, go the Properties section and change the value in the Text field. For our buttons we want to name them 'Go' and 'Clear'.

We should perhaps save this as we go along so we don't lose our work. File – Save from the menu bar of the Scene Builder application will take care of that for us.

We can now take a look at what our user interface will look like by using the preview feature in Scene Builder, go to the menubar and select 'Preview – Show Preview in Window'. You should see something like this:

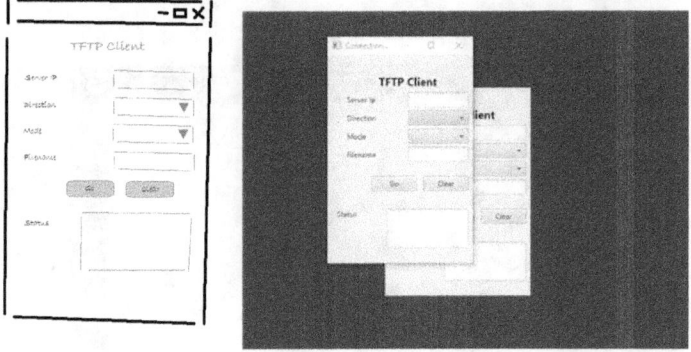

Figure 9 preview of user interface compared to original sketch

For now we will leave the FXML Document here and turn our attention to some Java.

Launching our App

As with all Java we need a class that is our launch point for our application and we will call ours *ClientTFTP* and place this in the '*softwarepulse.fx*' package, one level above our FXML Document. It is not important where it is placed I just want to be clear where I'm placing mine. To create the class we can right click on the package we already have and then select 'New – Class'. When the new class dialog appears change the package entry from '*softwarepulse.fx.view*' to '*softwarepulse.fx*' and then type the class name '*ClientTFTP*'. As we will use this class to launch our JavaFX application we will need to extend our class from the '*javafx.application.Application*' class, so set the Superclass field to this. Check the box to say we want a main method and that's all we need so press the finish button.

Figure 10 creating ClientTFTP class using wizard

In our *main()* method we will make a call to the *launch()* method passing the array of arguments passed to the main method. The launch method is defined in the Javafx.Application class which our ClientTFPT class has extended. This is not the only method to invoke the JavaFX application but is nice and simple for what we are doing.

The *launch()* method will then make a call to the *start()* method passing the entry point stage. The *start()* method is an abstract method declared in the *Application* class and therefore our *ClientTFTP* class will need to override that method and it is from here that we can add our items to the stage.

Our *start()* method is passed the primary stage and this we will assign to our class property *primaryStage*. We will also set the stage title. Next we will call a private method called *initRootLayout()* and as the name suggests we will create a starting layout for the application and add our FXML Document containing our items that we created earlier.

The *initRootLayout()* method creates a new FXMLLoader object which will allow us to load the FXML Document into the object and we do that by calling the *getResource()* method of our *ClientTFTP* class. We then call the *load()* method of the loader and assign the result into our *AnchorPane* class property.

With our *AnchorPane* object created and containing our group of items, we create a new scene using the *rootLayout* as a parameter. We can then add the scene to our *primaryStage* property. Finally, we show the stage and that renders our application to the display.

Our code for the *ClientTFTP* class looks like this:

```java
package softwarepulse.fx;

import java.io.IOException;
import javafx.application.Application;
import javafx.fxml.FXMLLoader;
import javafx.scene.Scene;
import javafx.scene.layout.AnchorPane;
import javafx.stage.Stage;

/**
 * @author jmcneil
 * @copyright (c) copyright Software Pulse 2017
 *
 */
public class ClientTFTP extends Application {

        private Stage primaryStage;
        private AnchorPane rootLayout;

        /**
         * @param args
         */
        public static void main(String[] args) {
                launch(args);
        }

        @Override
        public void start(Stage primaryStage) throws
Exception {
                this.primaryStage = primaryStage;
                this.primaryStage.setTitle("SP TFTP
Client");

                initRootLayout();
        }
```

```java
private void initRootLayout() {
    // Load root layout from fxml file.
    FXMLLoader loader = new FXMLLoader();

    loader.setLocation(ClientTFTP.class.getResource
            ("view/ConnectionOverview.fxml"));
    try {
        rootLayout = (AnchorPane)
loader.load();

        // Show the scene containing the root
layout.
        Scene scene = new Scene(rootLayout);
        primaryStage.setScene(scene);
        primaryStage.show();


    } catch (IOException e) {
            e.printStackTrace();
        }
    }

}
```

Now, when we run our code the user interface we produced earlier is displayed. Apart from closing the application we have no functionality and no options to select. We will now turn our attention to setting our options for our choice boxes and creating the code entry points for when the buttons are pressed.

Adding User Interface Controller

So far we have a main class which we use to launch our application and provide our basic user interface. We now need to add code to bridge the gap between our core application and our interface.

You may have come across the idea of code seperation, the idea that the view should be separate from the model and that there should be a control to manage the interchange between the view and model. What this is basically saying is that the code to display information should focus on how to display information. The code to manage the data and process should focus on that and there should be some code which knows how to pass the information between the two parties. The agument for this approach is that it allows changes to one part to be made without requiring changes to the other. We are essentially taking this approach here.

The next class we will build will be our controller class. Create a new class by right clicking on the package 'softwarepulse.fx.view'. Give the class the name 'ConnectionOverviewController' and press the finish button.

The first thing we will do is create names in our controller file for the fields we added to our FXML Document. We do this by adding an FXML tag '@FXML' and then on the next line we add private properties of the field type used in our interface. So for the 'file name' field it would be:

```
@FXML
private TextField fileNameField;
```

We will see shortly that by adding the @FXML tag we will be able to select these property names in Scene Builder when editing our FXML Document.

The other *@FXML* item we need to add is the *private initialize()* method (note the US spelling of the word). This method is automatically called after an FXML file is loaded where the FXML file specifies that this is the controller for the file. We will use this class to set up our options for choice boxes as well as a few other items.

The *initialize()* method will set the tool tip for each of the choice boxes, we will then use it to set the options for each of the choice boxes and then set the default value.

The last thing we will then do is set the focus for the cursor to be on the first field in the list; the Server IP field.

One thing I will say is that the setting of Choice box values has allegedly been problematic and people have in the past used work arounds to get the desired result. For this reason you will see that I clear out all the field options first before setting the new values. This approach works but should not be required and in newer versions may be supurflous.

The code for the controller is as follows:

```
package softwarepulse.fx.view;

import javafx.application.Platform;
import javafx.fxml.FXML;
import javafx.scene.control.ChoiceBox;
import javafx.scene.control.TextArea;
import javafx.scene.control.TextField;
import javafx.scene.control.Tooltip;

/**
 * @author jmcneil
 * (c) copyright Software Pulse 2017
 *
 */
public class ConnectionOverviewController {

    @FXML
    private TextField serverIPField;
    @FXML
    private ChoiceBox<String> modeField;
    @FXML
    private ChoiceBox<String> directionField;
    @FXML
    private TextField fileNameField;
```

```java
    @FXML
    private TextArea statusField;

    /**
     * Initializes the controller class. This method is
automatically
     * called
     * after the fxml file has been loaded.
     */
    @FXML
    private void initialize() {
        // Set the popup tool tip for the choice field
        modeField.setTooltip(new Tooltip("Select Ascii if
the file is text otherwise use binary"));

        modeField.getItems().removeAll(modeField.getItems(
));
        // Set the options for the field
        modeField.getItems().addAll("Ascii", "Binary");
        // By default select an option
        modeField.getSelectionModel().select("Binary");

        directionField.setTooltip(new Tooltip("Send (PUT)
or receive (GET))file from the server"));

        directionField.getItems().removeAll(modeField.getI
tems());
        directionField.getItems().addAll("GET", "PUT");
        directionField.getSelectionModel().select("GET");

        // Set the focus for the cursor to be the first
field at the top of
        // the scene
        // This is set after all the items are configured
and rendered.
        Platform.runLater(new Runnable() {
            @Override
            public void run() {
                serverIPField.requestFocus();
            }
        });
    }

}
```

Now if we go back to our FXML document, the ConnectionOverview file and open this in Scene Builder we can set the controller file to use. To do this we select the controller section on the left hand side of the screen and select ConnectionOverviewController as the Controller class name. Scene Builder automatically picks up all the classes that are contained within the same package, so if you have several classes in the same package as the FXML document then you will have more than one to select from. In our case we only have the one class.

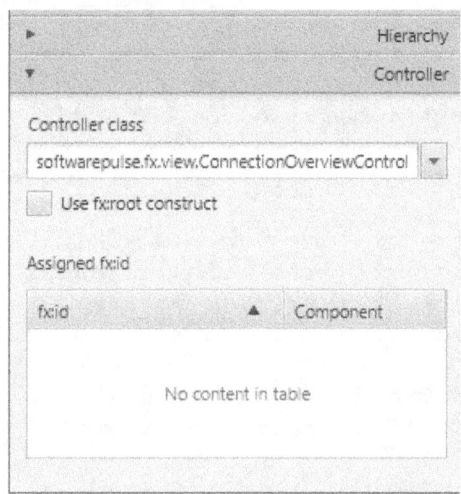

Figure 11 setting the controller class in Scene Builder

The next thing we need to do is to give names to our fields. These need to match up with those we defined in our controller class earlier. To set a field name, click on the field and then go to the Code section on the right hand side. The field 'fx:id' has a drop down list of field names which you should notice matche those fields defined earlier in our controller class. Select the name you want to use for that field. As names are selected the number of options for the other fields reduces to those still unused.

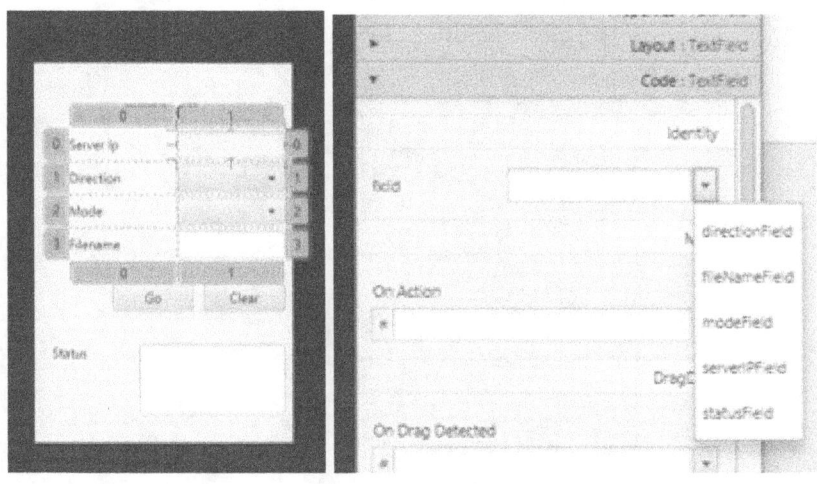

Figure 12 setting the field name

So we need to set the field names as follows:

Field label	Field name
Server Ip	serverIPField
Direction	directionField
Mode	modeField
Filename	fileNameField
Status	statusField

Save all that, then we are in a position to run our application. What we expect to see is our user interface. Each of our Choice Boxes to default to the values we have set and to display drop down options. The cursor should also be set to the Server IP field ready to receive input.

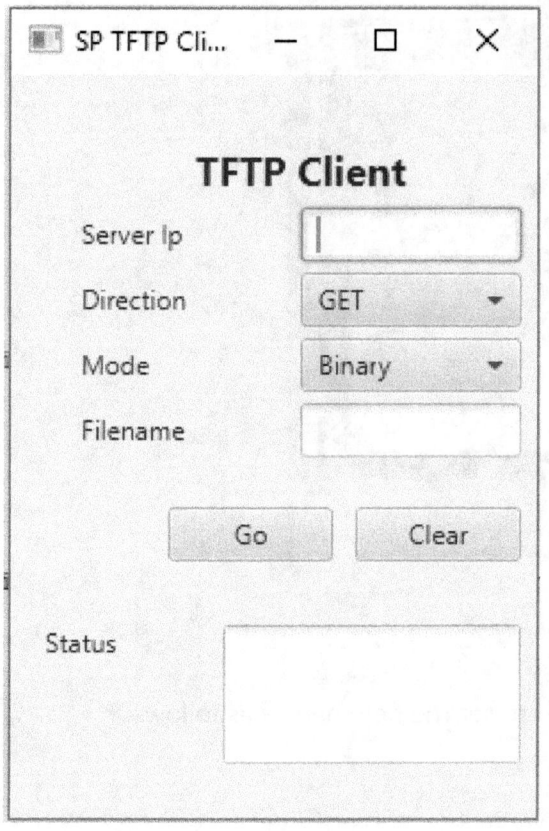

Figure 13 user interface with default values populated

Handling events

So now we have our user interface displaying our fields and our fields have options and default values where required the next thing to turn our attention to is the buttons.

We have two buttons on our UI, the 'Go' button which we will use to send our command to the designated TFTP server. The other button, the 'Clear' button will remove all values, including the default values from the input fields so we can enter a new command to a TFTP server.

Let's start with the Clear button. As we might expect the code for processing the Clear button is written in the controller class. We can then link our button object in our FXML document to the code in the controller much like we did for the field names.

Open up the *ClientOverviewController* class and we will add in a new method. The method will start with the '*@FXML*' tag which will tell Scene Builder that the method is available to link to an object in the scene. Next, we will define a private method called *handleClear()* which has no return and takes no parameters. Within this method we will set each of the field values to no data. The code for the method looks like this:

```
/**
 * Called when the user clicks clear.
 */
@FXML
private void handleClear() {
    serverIPField.setText("");
    modeField.valueProperty().set(null);
    directionField.valueProperty().set(null);
    fileNameField.setText("");
    statusField.clear();
}
```

If we save our controller class and then open the FXML document in Scene Builder we will be able to link our button to our new code. Select the Clear button and then go to the code section on the right-hand side. There you will see the 'On Action' field with a drop-down list of the methods defined within the controller class. We will select our new method *handleClear()* and save the changes.

If we run our application again and this time press the 'Clear' button we will notice that the Choice Box fields with their default values are set to no value. If we type into the other fields and the press the clear button the values in those fields are also cleared.

We now have our first button working, it's time to turn our attention to the 'Go' button.

The 'Go' button is intended to take the values the user enters and send these off to the TFTP server specified. For now, we will simply link our button to a method that later we can use to make the call to the TFTP server.

Once again we will go to our *ConnectionOverviewController* class and add a new method call *handleGo()*. On the line before the method signature will add the *@FXML* tag. For now, that is all we need. So, the code for the method looks like this:

```
/**
 * Called when the user clicks ok.
 */
@FXML
private void handleGo() {
}
```

Now we can open the FXML document in Scene Builder. Once open, click on the Go button and then in the in the Code section on the right-hand side of the application window select the 'On Action' drop down option. In the list of options, we should now be able to see 'handleGo'. Select this option and then save the changes.

That links both the buttons to our controller class, next we can build on this so we are able to make a call to the TFTP server.

Validating the fields

One of the checks we need to make before we make a call to our TFTP server is to ensure we have the information we require. Now all the fields on the application, with the exception of the Status field, are required to be completed to make a call to the server. We should at the very least check we have values for each field.

Go back to our *ConnectionOverviewController* class. Here we will add a new private method called *isInputValid()*. The method will return either true or false, true if all the fields pass validation and false if one or more of the fields fails validation.

As each field is checked, if the field fails validation a description of the failure will be added to a string variable within the method. The end of each failure message is terminated with a carriage return and line feed so that each message is displayed on a separate line.

The server IP field will be checked to see if the text associated with the field is of zero length or if there is no text currently associated with the field. So long as there is a least a single character the field passes validation. Now we know this is far from robust but for the purposes of demonstrating validation on the field this is what we will start with.

Next the Mode is checked, now because this field is a Choice box it can only have a value from one of the available options. Therefore we need only check that a value has been selected and we can do this using the *getValue()* method of the field. If *null* is returned, then nothing has been selected otherwise a value has been selected.

We take the same approach with the other two remaining fields, Direction and Filename.

After processing all the fields, if the error string has a zero-length string i.e. has no messages then, true is returned. If there are messages, then this means one or more fields failed validation.

To display the error messages, we create an *Alert* class passing it an *AlertType*, in this case an *AlertType* of error. The *Alert* title is set, some information text is added and finally the error string. The *Alert* box is displayed and remains open until the OK button is pressed. Whilst it is open it prevents access to the application.

The coded for our new method looks like this:

```
/**
 * Validates the user input in the text fields.
 *
 * @return true if the input is valid
 */
private boolean isInputValid() {
    String errorMessage = "";

    if (serverIPField.getText() == null ||
serverIPField.getText().length() == 0) {
        errorMessage += "No valid server IP!\n";
    }
    if (modeField.getValue() == null ) {
        errorMessage += "No valid mode!\n";
    }
    if (directionField.getValue() == null ) {
        errorMessage += "No valid direction!\n";
    }

    if (fileNameField.getText() == null ||
fileNameField.getText().length() == 0) {
        errorMessage += "No valid file name!\n";
    }

    if (errorMessage.length() == 0) {
        return true;
    } else {
        // Show the error message.
        Alert alert = new Alert(AlertType.ERROR);
        alert.setTitle("Invalid Fields");
        alert.setHeaderText("Please correct invalid
fields");
```

```
        alert.setContentText(errorMessage);
        alert.showAndWait();
        return false;
    }
}
```

Now we can go back to our *handleGo()* method we created earlier and make a call to the *isInputValid()* like this:

```
/**
 * Called when the user clicks ok.
 */
@FXML
private void handleGo() {
    if (isInputValid()) {

    }
}
```

When we run our application now if we press the Clear button to clear all the fields and then press the Go button, we see displayed all error messages for our input fields.

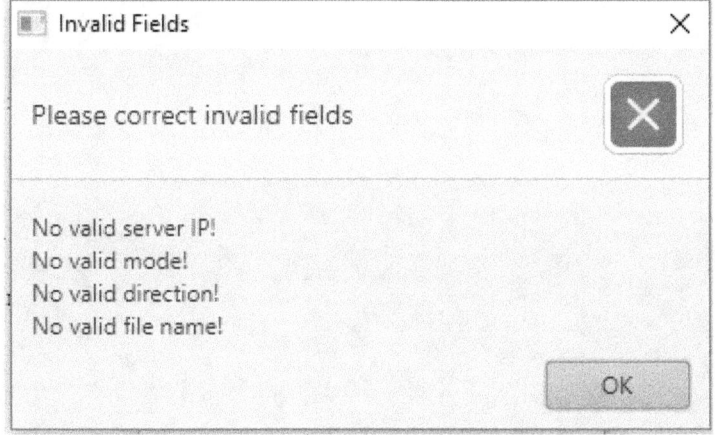

Figure 14 alert box showing error messages

Status Messages

There remains one more thing we need to do before we embark upon writing the code to interact with the TFTP server. The Status field is there to allow us to provide feedback to the user on progress of the file transfer. To get this to work we are going to use the event notification model used extensively throughout Java.

First off, we will create a new class called *MessageEvent* and have this extend the *EventObject*. The class will be placed in the '*softwarepulse.fx.event*' package. The constructor for this class will take an *Object* and a *String*. The *Object* will be the *Object* that fired the event and the *String* will be the message the object is passing to any objects registered as a listener.

The only other method will be the *getMessage()* method which listeners will use to retrieve the message passed. The *MessageEvent* class looks like this:

```java
package softwarepulse.fx.event;

import java.util.EventObject;

/**
 * @author jmcneil
 * (c) copyright Software Pulse 2017
 *
 */
public class MessageEvent extends EventObject {

        private String msg;

        public MessageEvent(Object source, String message)
{
                super(source);
```

```
        msg = message;
    }

    public String getMessage() {
        return msg;
    }
}
```

When we get around to building the code to manage the file transfer, we will take a look at how we generate these events. For now, what we need to do is put in place code within our controller so that it is capable of being notified of these events and can process them when they arrive.

We start by creating another new class, this time we will create an interface class. Any class that wants to be capable of being notified of message events should ideally implement this interface. We will place this class alongside our *MessageEvent* class so, in the package *'softwarepulse.fx.event'*. We will call the class *MessageListener* and it will define a single method signature of *sendMessage(MessageEvent)*.

The code for our interface is as follows:
```
package softwarepulse.fx.event;

/**
 * @author jmcneil
 * (c) copyright Software Pulse 2017
 *
 */
public interface MessageListener {
    void sendMessage(MessageEvent msg);
}
```

With these two classes in place we can now go back to our *ConnectionOverviewController* class and say that the class implements the *MessageListener* interface as follows:
```
public class ConnectionOverviewController implements
MessageListener {
```

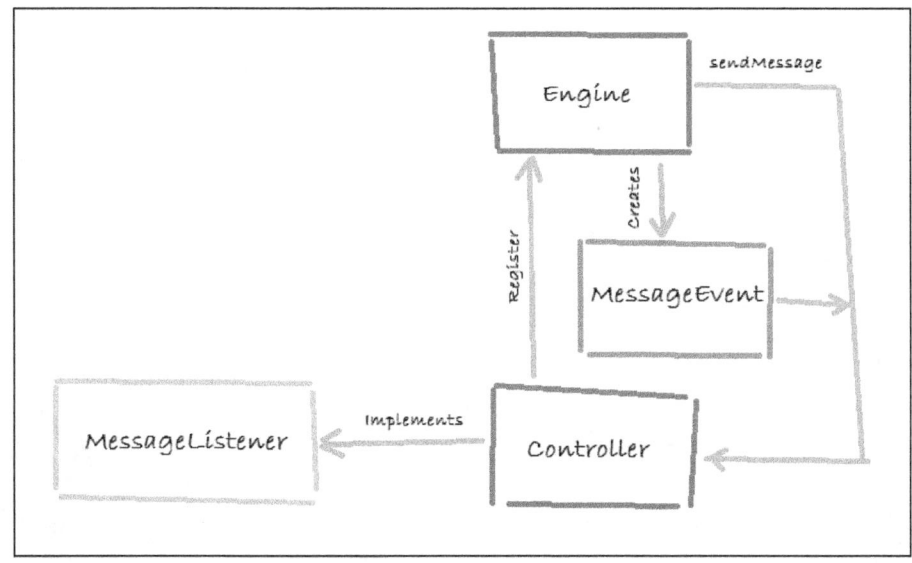

Figure 15 relationship between objects

We then have to add a new method, that of the method defined in the interface 'sendMessage()'. Within the method we will append to the Status field the contents of the message received as part of the *MessageEvent*. The code for the method is this:

```java
@Override
public void sendMessage(MessageEvent msg) {

statusField.appendText(msg.getMessage() + "\n");
}
```

We are now ready to start building the code to manage the file transfer with the server.

Managing the File Transfer

Whilst a Trivial File Transfer Protocol is simple there are still a lot of parts we need to pull together to successfully transfer files to and from a server. We will break these things down into smaller parts and walk our way through them.

First off, let us examine the basic approach and structure we plan to take.

We will build one class to hold all the code which handles transfer of files, not the best approach for ease of maintenance but it does keep all the code in one place. There will be a series of methods linked together in a chain.

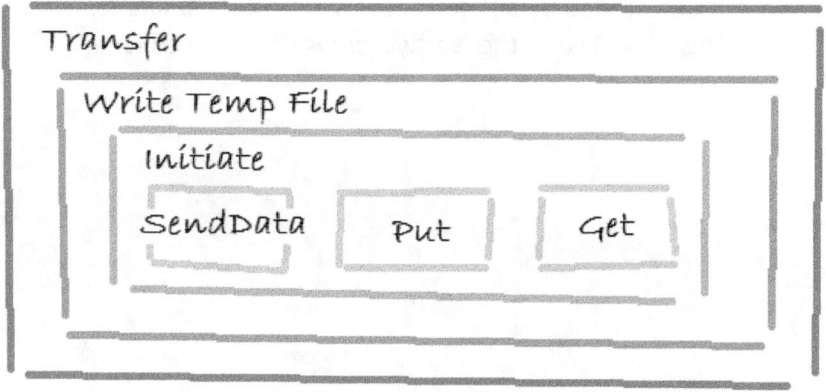

Figure 16 engine class flow of control

The entry point will be the *transfer()* method into which we will pass the connection information from our user interface. This in turn will call the *writeTempFile()* method.

We make use of temporary files when sending a file to the server to allow us to convert it from ASCII on our machine to NetASCII as required by TFTP. We also use temporary files when receiving a file from the server to build up the complete file. Once the complete file has been transferred, we then rename it to the target name. This avoids the risk of some other process trying to access the file before the transfer is complete.

The *writeTempFile()* in turn calls the *initiate()* method. The *initiate()* method makes a connection to the server and negotiates port numbers to complete the transfer. Finally, the *initiate()* method calls the method to either send a file to the server or receive a file from the server.

As each method concludes we cascade back through the preceding methods until we get back to the *transfer()* method which concludes the file transfer.

This approach allows us to ensure we close any files and sockets we open. The way it is structured means if a method opens a file or socket it is then responsible for closing it before exiting. If we encounter an error or exception and therefore need to terminate, we will still cascade back through the various methods closing the files and sockets as we go.

So, now we have an approach, we can start to build our class. This will of course be a new class and we will call it *Engine*. Not a great name but if you have a better idea by all means use your own naming convention. We will place this new class in the *'softwarepulse.fx.tftp'* package.

Generating Messages

With our new *Engine* class created the first thing we will do is put in place a means of generating message events. If you recall, we implemented the *MessageEvent* interface in our controller class. What we need to do now is have our *Engine* class generate events.

As you may be aware, it is usual to have means to add and remove event listeners to a class that generates events. As our class will generate events, we need to have a means of adding and removing objects which are capable of processing these events.

All objects which register as listeners for message events will be added to our *msgListener* list. In our class let us create a class property called *msgListener* of type *List* and assign it a new *ArrayList* object. This allows us to add and remove objects from the list as and when objects request to join or leave.

Next we need add two methods, both public, one called *addMsgListener()* and the other called *removeMsgListener()* which add and remove *MessageListener* objects.

To generate an event we will call the *fireMsgEvent()* method. This is a private method which is passed a message as string. This message is then encapsulated into the event object which is then sent out to all the listeners.

The *fireMsgEvent()* creates a new object of type *MessageEvent* passing to the constructor the text message received as a parameter. We then iterate through our list of objects registered as listeners and call the *sendMessage()* method of each listener. We know each listener has the method *sendMessage()* because each listener implements the *MessgeListener* interface which requires this method to be implemented.

With all that in place we are ready to send messages to any object that is interested. The code for the class looks like this:

```java
package softwarepulse.fx.tftp;

import java.util.ArrayList;
import java.util.Iterator;
import java.util.List;
import softwarepulse.fx.event.MessageEvent;
import softwarepulse.fx.event.MessageListener;

/**
 * @author jmcneil
 * (c) copyright Software Pulse 2017
 *
 */
public class Engine {

    private List<MessageListener> msgListeners = new
ArrayList<MessageListener>();

    /**
     * Class fires messages to provide information on
progress
     * any object wishing to be notified of progress
should
     * register as a listener using this method
     * @param l
     */
    public synchronized void addMsgListener(
MessageListener l ) {
        msgListeners.add( l );
    }

    /**
     * Class fires messages to provide information on
progress
     * any object wishing to be removed from
notification should
     * remove themselves as a listener using this
method
     * @param l
     */
    public synchronized void removeMsgListener(
MessageListener l ) {
        msgListeners.remove( l );
```

```
        }

    /**
     * This method is called within the class to notify
     * listeners of progress and errors.
     * @param msg - the message to send to listeners.
     */
    private synchronized void fireMsgEvent(String msg) {
        MessageEvent msgEvt = new MessageEvent( this,
msg );
        Iterator<MessageListener> listeners =
msgListeners.iterator();
        while( listeners.hasNext() ) {
            ( (MessageListener) listeners.next()
).sendMessage(msgEvt);
        }
    }

}
```

Now we have a means of sending messages from our *Engine* class we can turn our attention to its primary purpose, the transfer of files.

Kicking off the file transfer

As we discussed earlier, the entry point for transferring files will be the *transfer()* method. So, let us take a look at this.

The *transfer()* method is a public method which does not return a value. When calling the method, we will pass across the details for the connection to the server. We will take the parameters that are passed to the method and store them in class properties, so they are available for the other methods to use later. Finally, we will call the *writeTempFile()* method as the next method in the chain.

The parameters passed to the *transfer()* method are those required to initiate a call to the TFTP server, these would be the location of the server (IP), the file we are looking to transfer, are we sending or receiving the file (direction) and finally are we transferring as a binary file or as a text file and therefore using NetASCII (mode).

For the location of the server we will specify as an IP address and pass it as a *java.net.InetAddress* object. The file name we will pass as a simple *String* and the direction and mode will be passed as enumerators which we will have to define.

The enumerators for mode and direction are very simple, as each of these can only take one of two options. They allow us to ensure we pick a valid consistent option. The direction enumerator has options "GET" and "PUT" where "GET" is used to receive a file from the server and "PUT" is used to send a file to the server. The mode enumerator has the options "NETASCII" and "OCTET" where "OCTET" is used for the binary transfer.

We will also add private methods to allow the class properties to be set and retrieved. This allows us the opportunity put in place any validation the class may require on the properties or to add in change notification as required. In this example, we are not implementing any of this, but we have the setter methods in place should we wish to later.

So, we need to extend our *Engine* class with the following:

```java
    private List<MessageListener> msgListeners = new
ArrayList<MessageListener>();

        private InetAddress serverIp;
        private Direction dir;
        private Mode mode;
        private String fileName;

        public enum Direction {
            GET,
            PUT;
        }

        public enum Mode {
                NETASCII,
                OCTET;
        }

        /**
         * Entry point to initiate communication with a
server.
         * @param serverIp
         * @param direction
         * @param mode
         * @param file
         */
        public void transfer(InetAddress serverIp,
Direction direction, Mode mode, String file) {
                setServerIp(serverIp);
                setDir(direction);
                setMode(mode);
                setFileName(file);
                fireMsgEvent("Processing request");

                writeTempFile();
        }

        /**
         * Returns the server IP number
         * @return the serverIp
         */
```

```java
    private InetAddress getServerIp() {
        return serverIp;
    }


    /**
     * Sets the server IP number
     * @param serverIp the serverIp to set
     */
    private void setServerIp(InetAddress serverIp) {
        this.serverIp = serverIp;
    }

    /**
     * Returns the direction of transfer either
retrieve file
     * from server or send a file to the server
     * @return the dir
     */
    private Direction getDir() {
        return dir;
    }


    /**
     * Sets the direction of transfer either retrieve
file
     * from server or send a file to the server
     * @param dir the direction to set
     */
    private void setDir(Direction dir) {
        this.dir = dir;
    }


    /**
     * Return the mode of transfer either Netascii
     * or binary
     * @return the mode
     */
    private Mode getMode() {
        return mode;
    }
```

```java
/**
 * Set the mode of transfer either Netascii
 * or binary
 * @param mode the mode to set
 */
private void setMode(Mode mode) {
    this.mode = mode;
}




/**
 * Return the filename of the file to transfer
 * @return the fileName
 */
private String getFileName() {
    return fileName;
}




/**
 * Set the filename of the file to transfer
 * @param fileName the fileName to set
 */
private void setFileName(String fileName) {
    this.fileName = fileName;
}
```

Transfer using a temporary file

After the *transfer()* method the next method is the private method *writeTempFile()*. Whenever we do a transfer, we will use a temporary file. When we are sending a file up to the server, we will copy the file to a temporary file before sending to the server.

If we are sending the file as a text file, then we will convert the file from local text to NetASCII text and if using binary then we make a simple copy.

If we are receiving the file from the server then we write the data received from the server to the temporary file. Once the data has been sent down to the client, we will then convert from NetASCII to local ASCII if required and then rename the file to the target name.

So, the *writeTempFile()* method will create a temporary file name and then use this temporary file name to create a new *FileOutputStream* which we will then use to write the file data into.

If we encounter an error creating the output stream we throw an exception and exit the method. If we successfully create an output stream then we call the *initiateRequest()* method. Once the *initiateRequest()* returns then we close off the output stream and delete the temporary file.

To create the temporary file name, we will use the *File.createTempFile()* static method call. We pass the prefix "xxx-" and add an extension of ".tmp". This gives us a unique temporary file with a format similar to "xxx-nnnnnnnnnn.tmp".

The code for this new method and the additional class properties look like this:

```
        private static final String ERROR_WRITTING_FILE =
                    "Error writing to file.
Terminating.";
```

```java
        private static final String ERROR_CLOSING_FILE =
                "Error closing file.";

    File tempFile;
    FileOutputStream fout;

    /**
     * Creates a temporary file to write to
     */
    private void writeTempFile() {

        // create file
        fireMsgEvent("Creating temporary file");

        try {
                tempFile = getTempFile(new
File(fileName));
                fout = new FileOutputStream( tempFile
);
        } catch (IOException e2) {
                // set error and return
                e2.printStackTrace();
                fireMsgEvent(ERROR_WRITTING_FILE);
                return;
        }

        initiateRequest();

        // close file
        try {
                fout.close();
        } catch (IOException e) {
                // set error
                fireMsgEvent(ERROR_CLOSING_FILE);
                e.printStackTrace();
        }

        fireMsgEvent("Delete temporary file");
        tempFile.delete();

    }

    /**
     * Creates a temporary file name.  Temporary file
names are used
```

```
       * to convert NETASCII files into TFTP standard
before transmitting
       * and to receive files from server before
renaming to final name.
       * @param source java.io.File
       * @return java.io.File
       * @throws IOException
       */
     protected synchronized File getTempFile(File
source) throws IOException {
          File temp = File.createTempFile("xxx-",
"tmp");

          return temp;
     }
```

Initiate the request

We are now ready to make a call to the server and agree ports for the rest of the transfer. This is handled in the *initiateRequest()* method.

In this method, we will pick a port to use for the client side of the conversation. Also, we will set the port to use for the server side of things.

In order to call the server, we need to pass our request in the correct format. To do this we build a byte array containing the information for the connection. We then place this in a data packet and set the server IP address and default port. This data packet is then sent to the server and then the socket is closed.

The server has now been sent the connection request and now knows the port we will be listening on for a response. The listening part is handled by the *processGetRequest()* or *processPutRequest()* which we will call based on the setting of the direction property.

Now we have an idea of what we are trying to achieve in this section let us look at how we build up the code.

The first thing we will do is decide what port we are going to use for the conversation with the server. We will do this with a call to a private method called *getPort()* and we will pass to it an array of integers.

The array of integers contains all the possible port values we could use. We will define these values as a private integer array which we will call *port_range*. This allows us to change the range of available ports at the top of the class rather than having to trawl through the whole class to find where they are set.

Once we know the port we assign this to a *java.net.DatagramSocket*. This is another class level property which we will call '*server*' ready to use later.

We also need a property to hold the server port. Initially this will be set to the default TFTP server port but once we receive data from the server this will change to the port selected by the server to complete the conversation. To set the property we will again use a private *setServerPort()* method and pass an integer containing the port number.

Once the ports are set, we can then build our byte array containing the connection request. We achieve this by creating a private method *buildReq()* which returns a byte array and takes as parameters the file name and the mode.

Earlier on we took a look at how to build a request, the first two bytes determine if it is GET or PUT. This is added to a *ByteArrayOutputStream* which we will use to build up all the parts. Using the *ByteArrayOutputStream* allows us, once all the parts are added, to convert the contents into a single byte array.

Next, we get the file name as an array of bytes. A *null* is then added, followed by the mode and finally another *null*. This is all converted to a byte array which is then returned

The result of our *buildReq()* method call is then passed to another method *buildDatagramPacket()*. This is a private method which does not return a value and takes the byte array as a parameter.

The method creates a new *DatagramPacket* which is set with the byte array, the server IP address and the server port to use. The *DatagramPacket* is then sent and the socket connection closed.

Although the request may have failed to get through to the server, or it may have some other issue, we do not check at this point. If the request is successful, then when we listen on the port provided to the server, we should receive a message from the server. If there is no server message, then we will time out and close the connection.

So, having sent the request we now call *processPutRequest()* method if we want to send a file to the server or *processGetRequest()* method if we want to receive a file.

The additional code for the *Engine* looks like this:

```java
        private static final String PUT_DATA = "Sending
data to server.";
        private static final String GET_DATA = "Getting
data from server.";
        private static final String ERROR_SENDING_PACKET =
                "Error sending data packet to the server.";
        private static final String ERROR_STREAMING_DATA =
                "Unable to stream data";
        private static final String
ERROR_GETTING_SERVER_CONNECTION =
                "Error getting connection to server";
        private static final String ERROR_FILE_NOT_FOUND =
"File not found";
        private static final String
ERROR_WRITE_TO_TEMP_FILE =
                "Write to temp file";
        private static final String ERROR_READING_PACKET =
                "Reading data packet";
        private static final String
ERROR_SERVER_REPORTED_ERROR =
                "Server reported error";


        // TFTP servers listen on port 69 for connections
        public static final int SERVER_DEFAULT_PORT = 69;


        // TFTP Client Ports to use - use ports 49152 to
65535 to
        // avoid 'well known' ports.
        private int[] port_range = new int[]
                { 50152, 50153, 50154, 50155, 50156, 50157,
50158 };

        private DatagramSocket server = null;
        private int serverPort;
        private int clientPort;
        private DatagramPacket packetOut = null;
        private FileInputStream fin;
        private DatagramPacket packetIn;


        /**
        * Passed an array of integers, loops through each
```

```
      * looking for a free port with which to create a
      * datagram socket with. Returns the datagram socket
when
      * the first port is found.  if not port found
throws an exception.
      * @param ports
      * @return
      * @throws IOException
      */
    private DatagramSocket getPort(int[] ports) throws
IOException {
        for (int port : ports) {
            try {
                return new DatagramSocket(port);
            } catch (IOException ex) {
                continue; // try next port
            }
        }

        // if the program gets here, no port in the
range was found
        throw new IOException("no free port found");
    }


    /**
     * Returns the server port number
     * @return the serverPort
     */
    private int getServerPort() {
        return serverPort;
    }


    /**
     * Sets the server port number
     * @param serverPort the serverPort to set
     */
    private void setServerPort(int serverPort) {
        this.serverPort = serverPort;
    }

    /**
     * Builds a byte array with a TFTP server request
instruction
     * @param fileName
```

```java
     * @param transMode
     * @return byte array containing the request
     * @throws IOException
     */
    private byte[] buildRrq(String fileName, Mode
transMode) throws IOException {
        byte[] header = new byte[2];

        // GET is "01" and PUT is "02"
        header[0] = 0x00;
        if(dir == Direction.GET) {
            header[1] = 0x01;
            fireMsgEvent(GET_DATA);
        } else {
            header[1] = 0x02;
            fireMsgEvent(PUT_DATA);
        }

        // Use output stream to join various part of
the message
        ByteArrayOutputStream outputStream =
            new ByteArrayOutputStream( );
        outputStream.write( header );
        outputStream.write( fileName.getBytes() );
        outputStream.write( 0x00 );
        outputStream.write(
transMode.toString().getBytes() );
        outputStream.write( 0x00 );

        // Convert output stream to byte array
        byte[] result = outputStream.toByteArray();
        outputStream.close();
        return(result);
    }

    /**
     * Builds a Datagram packet using the byte array
passed
     * and assigns it to packetOut.
     * @param buf
     */
    private void buildDatagramPacket(byte[] buf) {
        packetOut = new
            DatagramPacket(buf, buf.length,
serverIp, serverPort);
```

```java
        }

    /**
     * Sends a packet of data to the server using the contents
     * of packetOut
     * @return
     */
    private boolean sendData() {

        try {
            server.send(packetOut);
            fireMsgEvent("Connected");
        } catch (IOException e) {
            // set error
            fireMsgEvent(ERROR_SENDING_PACKET);
            e.printStackTrace();
            return false;
        }
        return true;
    }

    /**
     * Makes the initial request to the server and calls the
     * GET or PUT process method
     */
    private void initiateRequest() {

        // connect to server
        fireMsgEvent("Connecting to server...");

        try {
            server = getPort(port_range);
            clientPort = server.getLocalPort();

            setServerPort(SERVER_DEFAULT_PORT);

            try {

buildDatagramPacket(buildRrq(fileName, mode));
                sendData();
                server.close();
```

```java
        if(getDir().name().equals("GET")) {
                        processGetRequest();
                } else {
                        processPutRequest();
                }

            } catch (IOException e) {
                // Close the server connection
created above
                server.close();
                // set error and return

    fireMsgEvent(ERROR_STREAMING_DATA);
                e.printStackTrace();
                return;
            }

        } catch (IOException e) {

    fireMsgEvent(ERROR_GETTING_SERVER_CONNECTION);
            e.printStackTrace();
        }
    }
```

Sending files to the server

If we have chosen to send a file to the server then the *initiateRequest()* method will make a call to the *processPutRequest()* method. This private method takes no parameters and does not return a value.

In the last method, *initiateRequest()*, we sent a call to the server. We now need to wait and listen for a response from the server to tell us what port we should use to continue the transfer conversation.

The approach we take for sending files to the server is as follows:

Open the file we wish to send to the server. If this file is to be sent as netascii then as we read the data from the file, convert it to netascii and write it to the temporary file. If the transfer is binary, then we simply read the data and write to the temporary file.

We then create a new datagram socket, setting the port to that of the client port we have selected. We also set the time out value. The time out value determines how long we will wait for a response before we give up. I have picked 10,000 milliseconds but you can select any value you think is suitable.

Now we have our socket created that is listening on the client port we told the server to use, we can use this to access any data sent to us by the server by calling the *receive()* method of the socket. The *receive()* method is what is known as a blocking method. That means that the code stops processing until it receives data from the source. Obviously if the server never responds then we would be stuck. This is where the timeout comes into play; if the timeout is reached without any communication then the code will throw a *SocketTimeout* exception.

As a result of the call we will place any packet received into a new Datagram Packet which will contain a byte array with the data we are looking for.

When the server responds and sends data to the client, the datagram socket receives the information. The data from the server will also contain the IP address and port number the server would like us to use to continue the conversation. We extract this information and save it to use later.

So long as we received a datagram packet, we can then parse the byte array. At this stage what we are looking for is the block counter. As you will no doubt recall, if we are sending a file to the server then the first block the server sends to us is zero '0'.

To prepare for transferring the file to the server we open the temporary file using a *FileInputStream*.

We then enter a loop and will continue to loop round until either the file transfer is complete, or an error occurs.

As we loop round, we check to see that the block number received from the server is the expected value. If it is not, then we resend the last packet to the server, so it knows what the last packet was we received and to send us the next in sequence.

If the block is as expected then we increment the block counter and call a method to build a byte array containing the TFTP operation code for DATA, the next sequence of block number and up to 512 bytes of data from the temporary file via our *FileInputStream* we opened earlier. What we get returned is a byte array.

We then call another method to build a datagram packet using the byte array. The datagram packet is addressed to point at the TFTP server using the port number it is expecting for the remainder of the transfer. A check is made to see if the byte array contained by the datagram packet is less than 512 bytes and therefore signals this is the last packet of data for the file. If this is the last packet, then the flag used to continue looping is set to false.

The packet of data is then sent to the server by calling the *sendData()* method. We then once again call the *readData()* method to access the server response. We once again check to see that the message received from the server is not an error message and read the block from the data packet.

So long as the flag is set to continue looping, we continue to read data from our file and send it to the server. Once all the data has been transferred, or an error is received from the server the server datagram socket is closed.

We then drop through all the chained methods closing off any open files and sockets and deleting temporary files.

That is how our code will handle the transfer when sending a file to the server.

Ok, the first thing we should cover off here is a class called *DataPacket*. This class was originally developed for a TFTP server but I have reused it here as well.

```java
package softwarepulse.server;

import java.util.Arrays;
import org.apache.logging.log4j.LogManager;
import org.apache.logging.log4j.Logger;

/**
 * @author jmcneil
 * (c) copyright Software Pulse 2017
 *
 * Contains the constituent parts of a TFTP Datagram
Packet
 */
public class DataPacket {

        private static final Logger logger =
                LogManager.getLogger(DataPacket.class);

        public final static String RRQ = "01";
        public final static String WRQ = "02";
        public final static String DATA = "03";
        public final static String ACK = "04";
        public final static String ERR = "05";

        public static final int MAX_DATA_SIZE = 512;

        protected byte[] data = new byte[0];
        private String errorMsg;
```

```java
    private String opCode;
    private String mode;
    private String filename;
    private int block;
    private int errCode;


    /**
     * Create object by passing byte array.
     * First two bytes are used to identify opCode
     * and the remaining byte array is parsed based on
the
     * opCode.
     */
    public DataPacket(byte[] data) {
        super();

        if(data.length >= 2) {
            logger.debug("Parsing op code");

            // first two bytes will be the
operation code
            Integer code1 = new Integer(data[0]);
            Integer code2 = new Integer(data[1]);

            opCode = new String(code1.toString() +
code2.toString());

            logger.debug("Checking for op code: "
+ opCode);

            switch(opCode) {
                case RRQ:
                    parseRRQ(data);
                    break;
                case WRQ:
                    parseWRQ(data);
                    break;
                case DATA:
                    parseDATA(data);
                    break;
                case ACK:
                    parseACK(data);
                    break;
                case ERR:
```

```java
                                        parseERR(data);
                                        break;
                              default:
                                        logger.error("Invalid
opCode: " + opCode);
                                        throw new
IllegalArgumentException
                                                ("Invalid opCode: "
+ opCode);
                    }
          } else {
                    logger.error("Invalid byte array
length: " +
                              data.length);
                    throw new IllegalArgumentException
                              ("Invalid byte array length: " +
data.length);
          }
    }


    /**
     * Parses Read Request byte array
     * 0-1 opCode
     * 2-x (terminated by 0x00)
     * x-y (terminated by 0x00)
     * @param data
     */
    private void parseRRQ(byte[] data) {
          logger.debug("Parsing RRQ");

          int posEndOfFilename = -1;
          int posEndOfMode = -1;

          int i;

          for( i=2; i<data.length; i++) {
                posEndOfFilename = i;
                if(data[i] == 0x00) {
                        break;
                }
          }

          setFilename(new
String(Arrays.copyOfRange(data, 2, posEndOfFilename)));
```

```java
                for( i= posEndOfFilename+1; i<data.length;
i++) {
                        posEndOfMode = i;
                        if(data[i] == 0x00) {
                                break;
                        }
                }

            setMode(new String(Arrays.copyOfRange(data,
posEndOfFilename+1, posEndOfMode)));

        }

    /**
     * Parses Write Request byte array
     * 0-1 opCode
     * 2-x (terminated by 0x00)
     * x-y (terminated by 0x00)
     * @param data
     */
    private void parseWRQ(byte[] data) {
            logger.debug("Parsing WRQ");

            int posEndOfFilename = -1;
            int posEndOfMode = -1;

            int i;

            for( i=2; i<data.length; i++) {
                    posEndOfFilename = i;
                    if(data[i] == 0x00) {
                            break;
                    }
            }

            setFilename(new
String(Arrays.copyOfRange(data, 2, posEndOfFilename)));

            for( i= posEndOfFilename+1; i<data.length;
i++) {
                    posEndOfMode = i;
                    if(data[i] == 0x00) {
                            break;
                    }
```

```java
                }

                setMode(new String(Arrays.copyOfRange(data,
posEndOfFilename+1, posEndOfMode)));

        }

        /**
         * Parse Data Request byte array
         * 0-1 opCode
         * 2-3 block, the sequence number of data block
         * 4-x (up to 512 bytes)
         * @param data
         */
        private void parseDATA(byte[] data) {
                logger.debug("Parsing DATA");

                // set block value
                Integer code1 = new Integer(data[2]);
                Integer code2 = new Integer(data[3]);
                code1 = code1 << 8;
                block = code1 + code2;

                // set data
                setData(Arrays.copyOfRange(data, 4,
data.length));

        }

        /**
         * Parse Acknowledge Request byte array
         * 0-1 opCode
         * 2-3 block, the sequence number of data block
         * @param data
         */
        private void parseACK(byte[] data) {
                logger.debug("Parsing ACK");

                // set block value
                Integer code1 = new Integer(data[2]);
                Integer code2 = new Integer(data[3]);
                code1 = code1 << 8;
                block = code1 + code2;
        }
```

```java
    /**
     * Parse Acknowledge Request byte array
     * 0-1 opCode
     * 2-3 error code
     * 2-x (terminated by 0x00)
     * @param data
     */
    private void parseERR(byte[] data) {
        logger.debug("Parsing ERR");

        // set error code value
        Integer code1 = new Integer(data[2]);
        Integer code2 = new Integer(data[3]);
        code1 = code1 << 8;
        errCode = code1 + code2;

        // set data
        setErrorMsg(new
String(Arrays.copyOfRange(data, 4, data.length)));
    }


    /**
     * @param data the data to set
     */
    private void setData(byte[] data) {
        this.data = data;
    }


    /**
     * @param errorMsg the errorMsg to set
     */
    private void setErrorMsg(String errorMsg) {
        this.errorMsg = errorMsg;
    }


    /**
     * @param filename the filename to set
     */
    private void setFilename(String filename) {
        this.filename = filename;
    }
```

```java
/**
 * @param mode the mode to set
 */
private void setMode(String mode) {
    this.mode = mode;
}


/**
 * @return the data
 */
public byte[] getData() {
    return data;
}


/**
 * @return the errorMsg
 */
public String getErrorMsg() {
    return errorMsg;
}


/**
 * @return the opCode
 */
public String getOpCode() {
    return opCode;
}


/**
 * @return the mode
 */
public String getMode() {
    return mode;
}


/**
 * @return the filename
 */
```

```java
public String getFilename() {
    return filename;
}


/**
 * @return the block
 */
public int getBlock() {
    return block;
}


/**
 * @return the errCode
 */
public int getErrCode() {
    return errCode;
}


/**
 * Check request is a read request
 * @return
 */
public boolean isRRQ() {
    if( getOpCode() != null) {
        if(getOpCode().equals(RRQ)) {
            return true;
        }
    }
    return false;
}


/**
 * Check request is a write request
 * @return
 */
public boolean isWRQ() {
    if( getOpCode() != null) {
        if(getOpCode().equals(WRQ)) {
            return true;
        }
    }
```

```java
        return false;
    }

    /**
     * Check the request is an Acknowledgement
     * @return
     */
    public boolean isACK() {
        if ( getOpCode() != null) {
            if (getOpCode().equals(ACK)) {
                return true;
            }
        }
        return false;
    }

    /**
     * Check the request is an Error
     * @return
     */
    public boolean isERR() {
        if ( getOpCode() != null) {
            if (getOpCode().equals(ERR)) {
                return true;
            }
        }
        return false;
    }


    // Can add other checks as required.
}
```

The class has a number of *public final static Strings* to represent one of each of the TFTP operation codes supported. There is also a public final static value for the maximum size of the data that can be passed at a time.

Then there are a number of class properties, one for each element that can be found in the collection of TFTP messages. Each one of these properties has a private setter method meaning that only methods within the class can set these and public getter methods so that the values can be accessed from outside the class.

This class is designed to take a byte array as a parameter when constructed. The first two bytes of the array are parsed and then the other methods allow the data contained in the byte array to be interrogated. It is designed to handle all the operation code messages sent in a TFTP conversation.

The two key methods we will use here are *isERR()* which returns true or false depending on if the operation code message was an error message.

The other method is *getBlock()* which returns an integer containing the block number for the message processed.

There is one more class that we will use that once again we have borrowed from the TFTP server implementation and this is the *DataParser* class. We only use this class to get the values for End Of File markers in the text files. This class provides the value to use for TFTP transfers and also the value to use for the local system we are currently running.

```java
package softwarepulse.server;

import java.io.ByteArrayOutputStream;
import java.io.IOException;
import java.util.Arrays;
import org.apache.logging.log4j.LogManager;
import org.apache.logging.log4j.Logger;

/**
 * @author jmcneil
 * (c) copyright Software Pulse 2017
 *
 */
public class DataParser {

        private static final Logger logger =
            LogManager.getLogger(DataParser.class);

        public static final String SYSTEM_STRING_EOL =
            System.getProperty("line.separator");
        //public static final String SYSTEM_STRING_EOL =
"\r";
        //public static final String SYSTEM_STRING_EOL =
"\n";
        public static final String TFTP_STRING_EOL =
"\r\n";
```

```
        public static final byte[] FILE_NOT_FOUND = {0x00,
0x05,  0x00,  0x01,
                    0x46,  0x69,  0x6c,  0x65,  0x20,
                    0x6E,  0x6F,  0x74,  0x20,
                    0x66,  0x6F,  0x75,  0x6E,  0x64,  0x00};
        public static final byte[] FILE_EXISTS = {0x00,
0x05,  0x00,  0x06,
                    0x46,  0x69,  0x6c,  0x65,  0x20,
                    0x61,  0x6C,  0x72,  0x65,  0x61,  0x64,
0x79,  0x20,
                    0x65,  0x78,  0x69,  0x73,  0x74,  0x73,
0x00};
        public static final byte[] NOT_DEFINED = {0x00,
0x05,  0x00,  0x00,
                    0x4E,  0x6F,  0x20,
                    0x6D,  0x6F,  0x72,  0x65,  0x20,
                    0x63,  0x6F,  0x6E,  0x6E,  0x65,  0x63,
0x74,  0x69,  0x6F,
                    0x6E,  0x73,  0x00};


}
```

Now we have the new classes out of the way, let us come back to our *processPutRequest()* method. The first thing we do is get our filename and get a *FileInputStream* handle to the file so that we can read the file contents. We do this by calling our getter method for file name and passing the result into the *openFile()* method. The *openFile()* method looks like this:

```
    /**
     * Creates and returns a FileInputStream from a
filename
     * @param filename
     * @return
     * @throws FileNotFoundException
     */
    private FileInputStream openFile(String filename)
throws FileNotFoundException {
            return new FileInputStream(filename);
    }
```

Once we have access to the file that we want to send we pass it into the private method *convertTextFile()* which takes the file input stream, the file output stream pointing to our temporary file and the enumerator for the direction we are sending the file. This method returns *true* or *false* to indicate if we were able to successfully convert the source file.

```java
    /**
     * Converts between netascii and local system ascii.
     * Uses direction to determine which way the
conversion should be.
     * The source file is the starting position and the
target file the result.
     * Required because Mac, Windows and Unix systems
use different End Of Line terminators.
     * @param source
     * @param target
     * @param d
     * @return
     */
    private boolean convertTextFile(FileInputStream
source,
            FileOutputStream target, Direction d) {

        fireMsgEvent("Converting to NETASCII...");

        DataInputStream dataIn = new DataInputStream(
source );
        BufferedReader bufferIn = new BufferedReader
            ( new InputStreamReader( dataIn ) );

        // Get a stream to write to the normalized file
        DataOutputStream dataOut = new DataOutputStream(
target );
        BufferedWriter bufferOut = new BufferedWriter
            ( new OutputStreamWriter( dataOut ) );

        String eol = null;
        if(d.equals(Direction.GET)) {
            eol = DataParser.SYSTEM_STRING_EOL;
        } else if(d.equals(Direction.PUT)){
            eol = DataParser.TFTP_STRING_EOL;
        }


        // For each line in the source file
        String line;
        try {
```

```
            while ( ( line = bufferIn.readLine() ) !=
null )
            {
                // Write the original line plus the
newline marker
                bufferOut.write( line );
                bufferOut.write( eol ); // write EOL
marker
            }

            // Close buffered reader & writer:
            bufferIn.close();
            bufferOut.close();
        } catch (IOException e) {
            // TODO Auto-generated catch block
            fireMsgEvent(ERROR_WRITE_TO_TEMP_FILE);
            e.printStackTrace();
            return false;
        }

        fireMsgEvent("Converted to NETASCII.");
        return true;
    }
```

To convert the text file both the source and the target *FileInputStreams* are accessed using a *BufferRead* and *BufferWriter* respectively.

A check is then made to see if we are sending the file to the server or receiving. If we are receiving, then we want to change the End Of Line (EOL) marker in the file from the standard TFTP version used to send us the file to whatever our local system uses. We work this out using a call to Java to get the value from the system we are running the JVM on. This way we can move our code between machine architectures and it will still work.

As we are sending, we loop through the source file reading a line at a time. By reading a line at a time we get the line of text but not the EOL marker. Therefore, when we write the line to the target file there is no EOL marker present. We then write our own EOL marker suitable for our audience. In this case we are sending to the TFTP server, so we would write the TFTP EOL marker to the file.

Once all the lines have been read and then written to the target file, our temporary file, we then close our buffers and signal success to the invoker.

We have now laid the groundwork ready to send the file. Having sent a request to the server it is time to listen for a response.

Each time the server sends us a message we need to read the information. To do this we have a *readData()* method which takes no parameters and returns *true* or *false* to indicate if the action was successful.

```
/**
 * Reads a packet of data from the server
 * @return boolean
 */
private boolean readData() {

        byte[] buf = new
byte[DataPacket.MAX_DATA_SIZE+4];
        packetIn = new DatagramPacket(buf,
buf.length);

        try {
                server.receive(packetIn);
        } catch (IOException e) {
                // set error
                fireMsgEvent(ERROR_READING_PACKET);
                e.printStackTrace();
                return false;
        }
        return true;
}
```

We know that the server will send us data in not more than 512-byte chunks. Therefore, we create a byte array of 512 bytes by using *DataPacket.MAX_DATA_SIZE* and then we add on 4 bytes more to allow for the operator code and the block counter. This we wrap up into a datagram packet and then make a call to the receive method of the server datagram socket. If there is no error, then we return *true* otherwise we fire a message and return *false*.

The data packet we receive from the server is then passed into the constructor of the *DataPacket* class to give us an object containing all the component parts of the message. We can then use the *getBlock()* and *isERR()* methods to check that we received the correct information from the server in order to move on to the next packet.

We would expect the block to be zero the first time. So long as there is no error the temporary file is accessed with a *FileInputStream* so we can read the data. We then enter our loop that we will use until the file transfer is complete. In order to create the data to send to the server we make a call to *buildData()* method. This is similar to the *buildRrq()* method we used earlier to build the request. The *buildData()* method takes the next *blockCounter* in the sequence as a parameter.

```java
/**
 * Builds a byte array containing data from the
source file
 * @param counter
 * @return byte array containing data message
 * @throws IOException
 */
private byte[] buildData(int counter) throws
IOException {
        byte[] data = new
byte[DataPacket.MAX_DATA_SIZE];
        byte[] header = new byte[4];
        int bytesRead;

        // DATA is "03"
        header[0] = 0x00;
        header[1] = 0x03;

        // Should really throw an error if counter
exceeds
        // 4 bytes, 65,535
        if(counter < 256) {
                header[2] = 0x00;
                header[3] = new
Integer(counter).byteValue();
        } else {
                header[2] = new Integer((counter &
0xFF00) >> 8).byteValue();
                header[3] = new
Integer(counter).byteValue();
        }

        // Request to read from the file the number
of bytes in 'data'
```

```
            // Find out how many bytes were actually
read, may be less
            // than size of data
            bytesRead = fin.read(data);

            // Use the output stream to concatenate the
two byte arrays
            ByteArrayOutputStream outputStream =
                new ByteArrayOutputStream( );
            outputStream.write( header );
            // Only write the number of bytes read. The
rest of data is
            // filled with NULL
            outputStream.write(data, 0, bytesRead);

            // Convert output stream into byte array
            byte[] result = outputStream.toByteArray();

            outputStream.close();

            return result;
    }
```

The *buildData()* method is used to build the final byte array that we will send to the server. The DATA message is built up using two arrays. The header array is 4 bytes long and is fixed in length. The first two bytes hold the operation code which in this case will be '03'. So, we simply set the first byte to '*0x00*'. The second byte is set to '*0x03*'. The first two characters '0x' are control characters and state that the following characters should be treated as a hexadecimal value. We then have '03' which is the integer number three in hexadecimal left padded with zeros, so '0000 0000 0000 0011' in binary.

The bytes 3 and 4 are set similarly. We check to see if the value of counter, the parameter passed to the method, is less than 256. If it is then we know the first byte will be zero. If it is not, then we need to convert the counter integer value to two bytes with the first byte holding the high order and the second byte holding the low order.

To do this we take the integer value we have, and we force all the bits that make up the low order byte to zeros. So, we start with our integer and we apply the 'AND' bitwise operator to the number by using '*& 0xFF00*'.

The ampersand is the bitwise 'AND' operator, the 0x tells the compiler the value following is hexadecimal, and the FF part of the hexadecimal number ensures all the high order bits of the number remain unchanged and finally the 00 following the FF ensures all the low order bits are forced to zero.

What we have now are the top 8 bits with a value and the lower 8 bits are all zero. Next, we shift all the bits to the right using '>> 8' so the 8 high order bits end up occupying the space that the low order bits held. The low order bits are discarded but that does not matter as we have already set them to zero. Now we have a new number which we convert to an Integer object and then to a byte which in turn is added to the byte array.

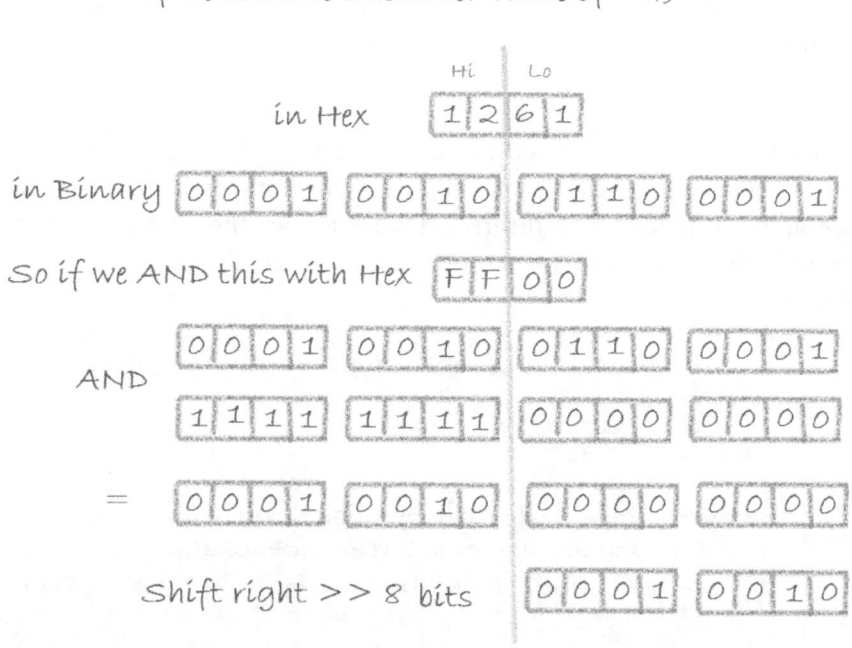

Figure 17 example of converting an integer to two bytes

For the low order byte we can simply create an Integer object from the counter, convert it to a byte using *byteValue()* and then assign it to the low order byte array. The high order part will be stripped off because there is no room to store it. That gives us the header.

Next, we read from our temporary file passing our data array as a parameter. This will return at most 512 bytes of data but may return less. We use the *bytesRead* variable to tell us how many bytes were actually read.

With both our arrays populated we now write the header and data arrays into a *ByteArrayOutputStream*. When writing the data array, we only want to write the number of bytes read in from the file so this is where we use the *bytesRead* variable to limit the number of bytes written to the stream.

Once all the information is written we then call the *toByteArray()* method of the stream to give us a single byte array containing the complete message. This byte array is then returned to the method which called it.

The next method involved in helping us send data to the server is the *private buildDatagramPacket()* method which takes a byte array as a parameter but does not return an object. As the name suggests this method creates a datagram packet which we can use to send to the TFTP server.

```
/**
 * Builds a Datagram packet using the byte array passed
 * and assigns it to packetOut.
 * @param buf
 */
private void buildDatagramPacket(byte[] buf) {
        packetOut = new DatagramPacket
        (buf, buf.length, serverIp, serverPort);

}
```

The method simply creates a new datagram packet using the byte array parameter passed to the method call. We will set the server IP number from the field *serverIP* and the port to talk to from the field *serverPort*. This new datagram packet we will assign to the field *packetOut* to use later.

The last of the methods involved in sending data to the server is the *private sendData()* method which takes no parameters and returns *true* or *false* to indicate if the packet was sent. This is the same method we saw earlier when running the *initiateRequest()* method.

```
    /**
     * Sends a packet of data to the server using the
contents
     * of packetOut
     * @return
     */
    private boolean sendData() {

            try {
                server.send(packetOut);
                fireMsgEvent("Connected");
            } catch (IOException e) {
                // set error
                fireMsgEvent(ERROR_SENDING_PACKET);
                e.printStackTrace();
                return false;
            }
            return true;
    }
```

All this method does is use the server socket connection we made earlier to call the *send()* method passing the *packetOut* object.

That takes care of all the supporting classes and methods we can now look at the *processPutRequest()* method which makes use of all these items. This method is another private method which takes no parameters and does not return an object.

```
    /**
     * Copies the file to transmit to a temp file and
then sends
     * the data in the file to the server.
     */
    private void processPutRequest() {

            // flag used to indicate when finished
processing file
            boolean running;
            // Counter used for retries to get same data
from server
            int retry;
            DataPacket dpRecd;
```

```java
        // data block received from server
        int block;
        // data block expected from server
        int blockCounter = 0;
        byte[] sendData;

        // write file data to temporary file
        try {
                fin = openFile(getFileName());
        } catch (FileNotFoundException e3) {
                fireMsgEvent(ERROR_FILE_NOT_FOUND);
                e3.printStackTrace();
                return;
        }
        fireMsgEvent("Reading file data into
temporary file...");

        // If transfer mode is binary then just do a
straight copy
        // of data.If we are using NETASCII then we
need to convert            // from native format to
netascii format.
        if(mode.equals(Mode.NETASCII)) {

                if(convertTextFile(fin, fout, dir)) {
                        try {
                                fin.close();
                                fout.close();
                        } catch (IOException e1) {

     fireMsgEvent(ERROR_CLOSING_FILE);
                                e1.printStackTrace();
                        }
                } else {
                        // Failed to convert text file
so back out
                        try {
                                fin.close();
                                fout.close();
                        } catch (IOException e1) {

     fireMsgEvent(ERROR_CLOSING_FILE);
                                e1.printStackTrace();
                        }
                        return;
```

```java
                    }
            } else {
                    // Binary transfer so simply copy data
to temp file
                    try {
                            int b = fin.read();
                            while(b != -1) {
                                    fout.write(b);
                                    b = fin.read();
                            }
                    } catch (IOException e) {

    fireMsgEvent(ERROR_WRITE_TO_TEMP_FILE);
                            e.printStackTrace();
                            try {
                                    fout.close();
                                    fin.close();
                            } catch (IOException e1) {

    fireMsgEvent(ERROR_CLOSING_FILE);
                                    e1.printStackTrace();
                            }
                            return;
                    }
            }
            fireMsgEvent("Data moved into temporary
file.");

            fireMsgEvent("Sending file to server...");
            try {
                    server = new
DatagramSocket(clientPort);
                    server.setSoTimeout(10000);
            } catch (SocketException e1) {

    fireMsgEvent(ERROR_GETTING_SERVER_CONNECTION);
                    e1.printStackTrace();
                    return;
            }

            if(!readData()) {
                    // readData() method has already
logged error message
                    server.close();
                    return;
```

```
                }

                setServerIp(packetIn.getAddress());
                setServerPort(packetIn.getPort());

                // read ack
                dpRecd = new DataPacket(packetIn.getData());
                block = dpRecd.getBlock();
                if(dpRecd.isERR()) {
                        // error requesting op from server

        fireMsgEvent(ERROR_SERVER_REPORTED_ERROR);
                        server.close();
                        return;
                }


                try {
                        fin = new FileInputStream(tempFile);
                } catch (FileNotFoundException e) {
                        fireMsgEvent(ERROR_FILE_NOT_FOUND);
                        server.close();
                        e.printStackTrace();
                }

                // keep processing data until we receive
less than
                // DataPacket.MAX_DATA_SIZE bytes of data
                running = true;
                retry = 0;              // clear the retry counter
                while(running) {
                        // If we do not receive the expect
block then re-send
                        // the last packet of data
                        // otherwise send the next packet of
data
                        if(block == blockCounter) {

                                blockCounter++;
                                // load next block of data
                                try {
                                        retry = 0;
                                        sendData =
buildData(blockCounter);
```

```java
        buildDatagramPacket(sendData);
                                // Check to see if we are
sending data of
                                // length
DataPacket.MAX_DATA_SIZE
                                // Note we add 4 bytes
because the packet has
                                // Op code and block added
to it
                                // If less than
DataPacket.MAX_DATA_SIZE then
                                // this is the last packet
of data
                                if(sendData.length <
(DataPacket.MAX_DATA_SIZE+4)) {
                                        running = false;
                                }
                        } catch (IOException e) {
                                running = false;

        fireMsgEvent(ERROR_STREAMING_DATA);
                                e.printStackTrace();
                                try {
                                        fin.close();
                                } catch (IOException e1) {

        fireMsgEvent(ERROR_CLOSING_FILE);

        e1.printStackTrace();
                                }
                                server.close();
                                return;
                        }
                } else {
                        retry++;
                        if(retry >= 3) {
                                running = false;
                        }
                }
                // send block of data
                sendData();
                readData();
```

```
                    dpRecd = new
DataPacket(packetIn.getData());
            block = dpRecd.getBlock();
            if(dpRecd.isERR()) {

    fireMsgEvent(ERROR_SERVER_REPORTED_ERROR);
                    running = false;
            }


        }

        fireMsgEvent("Transfer complete.");
        server.close();
        try {
            fin.close();
        } catch (IOException e) {
            fireMsgEvent(ERROR_CLOSING_FILE);
            e.printStackTrace();
        }


    }
```

First off, we need to open the source file for reading. This is the file we want to transfer up to the server. In the event we cannot open the file then we will fire an error message and drop out of the method.

Next, we will check to see how the file is to be transferred to the server. If we are going to transfer the file using netascii then we make a call to the *convertTextFile()* method we described earlier. Again, if this fails, we fire a message and drop out of the method.

If the transfer is using binary, then we loop through each byte of the file and write it to the temporary file.

We will then make a connection to the server by creating a new datagram socket, listening on the client port we told the server to use earlier on. As reading from the server is a blocking event, that means we will wait until there is something to read from the server, we will set a timeout to state how long we want to wait before we fail. For this we will use a value of 10,000 milliseconds.

Before we made a call to this method, we sent a datagram packet to the server to tell it to send messages to us at our IP address and on a specific port. What we will do now is listen on that port to see if we get a response from the server. We do this by making a call to the *readData()* method. If we fail to get a response before the time out, then we are going to drop out of the method.

Once we get a response from the server, we can find out what address and port the server wants us to continue using for the conversation. We set the *serverIP* and *serverPort* fields, so we can use them later.

Each time we receive a packet from the server we will create a new object of type *DataPacket* passing it the datagram packet received. Creating an object using this class allows us to easily obtain the block number sent by the server as well as call the *isERR()* method to see if the server sent an error message.

So long as there was no error in the message sent from the server, we then open the temporary file for reading using a *FileInputStream*. Then we are ready to start reading the data and sending to the server in a loop.

Before we go into the loop, we set the *running* flag to *true*. We will continue to loop until this flag is *false*. We also set the *retry* counter to zero. If the server sends a packet with the wrong block number, we will resend our last packet to the server asking for the next in sequence three times in a row. If after three attempts, we still have not received a packet with the correct block number then we will stop the transfer.

So, with those set, we set up a continuous loop. The first thing we check is that the block number we received matches the *blockCounter*. *BlockCounter* is used to track what we expect to receive from the server as the next block number.

If block fails to match *blockCounter* we increment the *retry* counter. If the *retry* counter is 3 or more then we set the *running* flag to *false* to stop the loop. If a match, then resend the data packet and wait to read a response.

The data packet received is then put into a *DataPacket* object and the block number obtained as well as a check to see if the server sent an error. We then re-enter the loop and do a block check once again.

If the *block* and *blockCounter* match, then we know that the data packet we have is the next in sequence. We increment the *blockCounter* as this is the next in the series we need to send up to the server and receive ACK in return.

We clear the retry counter as this is the first attempt at obtaining the new block of data. We then call *buildData()* and *buildDatagramPacket()* in succession to build up the data packet containing the file data to send to the server. A check is also made to see if the size of the *datapacket* is less than a full 512-byte packet. If it is less, then this signals that this is the last packet to send and we set the running flag to *false*, so we do not enter the loop again.

If there are no errors in pulling together the data packet we call the *sendData()* and *readData()* methods to transmit the packet to the TFTP server and await the server response before going back through the loop if the flag is still true.

Once out of the loop we fire off a message and then close the server socket connection. We can then drop through the chain of methods we called getting to the method closing off all the open files and sockets as required.

Receiving files from the server

If we have chosen to receive a file from the server then the *initiateRequest()* method will make a call to the *processGetRequest()* method. This private method takes no parameters and does not return a value.

The *processGetRequest()* call to the server is all about sending a file to the server. We send the initial request to the server for a connection. Then we need to wait and listen for a response from the server to tell us what port we should use to continue the transfer conversation.

The approach we take for this method is as follows:

Create a new socket connection and set the port we will use to listen for messages to that which we informed the server to use. We will also set a time out value on the socket connection; this is because when we read information from the server it is a blocking action, so we will wait until we receive something. Obviously, the server may never respond and then we would be left there waiting so, a time out is set and if we do not get a response within the time limit then we will throw an error. We will set the time out value to be 10,000 milliseconds, this is an arbitrary value and you can change this around to a value that suits you.

Once our socket for connecting to the server is in place then we make a call to read any data packet the server has sent to us.

Once the packet of data is received, we can then obtain the IP Address and port which the server wants us to use to continue the conversation.

The request we made to the server was to receive a file and therefore if the server can locate the requested file this first packet should contain the first part of the file. The block number should also be '01'.

So, once the first packet is received from the server, we create a continuous loop by setting the *'running'* flag to *true* and using this in a while loop. We then check the length of the packet received because although this is the first packet it may also be the last if the whole file fits within the 512 bytes sent.

Should the packet contain data of less than 512 bytes then we need to copy the number of bytes sent to a *ByteArrayOutputStream*. We do this because when we read data using the socket, we use a byte array of 512 bytes. If the server only sent us 10 bytes, the byte array would contain 10 bytes of data and the rest would be full of *null* bytes. If we now copy this to a file, we would in fact copy all 512 bytes, 10 bytes of data and the rest as nulls. This is not what we are after.

So, if we have less than 512 bytes, we create a new *ByteArrayOutputStream* and only copy the number of bytes the server sent.

Once we have either the 512 bytes or isolated the number of bytes sent, we put this into a new *DataPacket* object. We check there is no error. If an error is encountered, then we throw an error and exit the method.

If there is no error, then we check to see if the data length we received is less than 512 bytes. If less than 512 bytes this is a signal that we have reach the end of the file. We set the *'running'* flag to false so that we stop looping round reading data from the server.

We write the data out to the *FileOutputStream* which is pointing at our temporary file.

We then make a call to the private *buildAck()* method passing to it the block number from the last packet received from the server.

The *buildAck()* method creates and returns a byte array. This byte array contains the message to tell the server that we have received the packet it sent. From that the private method *buildDatagramPacket()* method is called passing the byte array. This method builds a new datagram packet containing the message to send to the server and then the private method *sendData()* is called to transfer the packet.

If the *'running'* flag is still set to *true*, then the next packet of data is read from the server and we go through the loop again.

Once the loop ends then the *FileOutputStream* is closed and the socket connection to the TFTP server is closed.

We now need to move the file from our temporary file to its final destination. Along the way we check to see if this was a netascii transfer. If it was a netascii transfer, then we open the temporary file and create a new file with the target destination and call our method for converting text end of line markers between systems. We finish off by closing the file streams.

If this is a binary transfer, then we simply rename the temporary File to the target file name.

We can then exit the method and drop down through the other methods we called along the way to close off any open files and sockets.

There is quite a bit of code associated with this section but less than the previous section mainly because we are reusing a number of methods we have already dealt with. So, let us look at how it is built up. Here is the code for the *processGetRequest()*:

```
/**
 * Reads in data from server writes to temp file
then
 * renames temp file to target file name
 */
private void processGetRequest() {

        boolean running = true;

        try {
                server = new
DatagramSocket(clientPort);
                server.setSoTimeout(10000);
        } catch (SocketException e1) {

        fireMsgEvent(ERROR_GETTING_SERVER_CONNECTION);
                e1.printStackTrace();
                return;
        }

        fireMsgEvent("Reading file...");
        if(!readData()) {
```

```java
                        // Error msg set in readData so just
return
                    server.close();
                    return;
            }

        setServerIp(packetIn.getAddress());
        setServerPort(packetIn.getPort());

        DataPacket dpRecd;

        while(running) {
                if(packetIn.getLength() <
(DataPacket.MAX_DATA_SIZE + 4)) {
                        ByteArrayOutputStream
tempOutputStream = new ByteArrayOutputStream();
                        if(packetIn.getLength() > 0) {
                                try {

    tempOutputStream.write(Arrays.copyOf(packetIn.getD
ata(), packetIn.getLength()));
                                } catch (IOException e) {

    fireMsgEvent(ERROR_STREAMING_DATA);
                                        server.close();
                                        e.printStackTrace();
                                        return;
                                }
                        }
                        dpRecd = new
DataPacket(tempOutputStream.toByteArray());
                } else {
                        dpRecd = new
DataPacket(packetIn.getData());
                }

                if(dpRecd.isERR()) {
                        // set error and return
                        running = false;
                        // Output the reason for the
error

    fireMsgEvent(ERROR_SERVER_REPORTED_ERROR + " : " +
dpRecd.getErrCode() + " - " + dpRecd.getErrorMsg() );
                        return;
```

```java
                } else {
                    if (dpRecd.getData().length <
DataPacket.MAX_DATA_SIZE) {
                        // end of file reached
                        running = false;
                    }
                    try {

    fout.write(Arrays.copyOf(dpRecd.getData(),
dpRecd.getData().length));
                    } catch (IOException e) {
                        running = false;
                        // set error and return

    fireMsgEvent(ERROR_STREAMING_DATA);
                        server.close();
                        e.printStackTrace();
                        return;
                    }
                }


    buildDatagramPacket(buildAck(dpRecd.getBlock()));

                if(!sendData()) {
                    running = false;
                }

                if(running) {
                    if(!readData()) {
                        running = false;
                    }
                }
            }

            // Close the file
            try {
                fout.close();
            } catch (IOException e) {
                fireMsgEvent(ERROR_CLOSING_FILE);
                e.printStackTrace();
            }

            server.close();
```

```java
        fireMsgEvent("File read");

        File tempFile2 = null;
        if(mode.equals(Mode.NETASCII)) {
            fireMsgEvent("Convert file from
NETASCII to system text...");

            // Convert temp file from NETASCII to
local system ascii
            // write data to temp file
            try {
                fin = new
FileInputStream(tempFile);
            } catch (FileNotFoundException e) {

    fireMsgEvent(ERROR_FILE_NOT_FOUND);
                e.printStackTrace();
                return;
            }

            try {
                tempFile2 = getTempFile(new
File(fileName));
                fout = new FileOutputStream(
tempFile2 );
                convertTextFile(fin, fout,
getDir());
                fout.close();
                fin.close();
            } catch (IOException e2) {
                // set error and return

    fireMsgEvent(ERROR_WRITTING_FILE);
                e2.printStackTrace();
                return;
            }
            fireMsgEvent("Converted");

        } else {
            tempFile2 = tempFile;
        }

        // rename temp file
```

```
        fireMsgEvent("Rename temp file to target
name...");
        tempFile2.renameTo(new File(fileName));
        fireMsgEvent("transfer complete.");

    }
```

Next thing we should cover off here is the *buildAck()* method. This method is designed to build a byte array containing the acknowledge message that we can send to the TFTP server.

```
/**
 * Build an ACK message
 * @param counter
 * @return byte array containing ACK message
 */
private byte[] buildAck(int counter) {
        byte[] header = new byte[4];

        // ACK is "04"
        header[0] = 0x00;
        header[1] = 0x04;

        // Should really throw an error if counter
exceeds
        // 4 bytes, 65,535
        if(counter < 256) {
                header[2] = 0x00;
                header[3] = new
Integer(counter).byteValue();
        } else {
                header[2] =
                        new Integer((counter & 0xFF00)
>> 8).byteValue();
                header[3] = new
Integer(counter).byteValue();
        }

        return header;
}
```

We pass the block number to the method when we make the call. This is the block counter we received in the last packet from the server. We send this same value back to the server so that the server knows which block of data we are acknowledging. Providing the ACK message contains the block number matching the last block sent by the server, the server will then send the next block.

The first thing we do is assign the first two bytes of our byte array to the operation code for acknowledge which is '04'.

Then we take the block number which, in the method we refer to as counter, and check to see if it is less than 256. If it is 255 or lower, then it can be represented with a single byte. If it is greater than 255 we will need to use two bytes and do the same as we did for the *buildData()* method when we were sending a file to the server.

The ACK is simpler than the data message so that is all the byte array needs to contain.

The Final Touch

The is just one last bit of code to put in place before we can use our Client and that is, we need to add the code to make a call to our engine. To do this we open up the *ConnectionOverviewController* class and go to the *handleGo()* method. All we have here at the moment is a call to our field validation method. We now need to create an engine object and pass to it the contents of our fields.

So the *handleGo()* method now looks like this:

```java
/**
 * Called when the user clicks ok.
 */
@FXML
private void handleGo() {
    if (isInputValid()) {
        // Call the TFTP server
        statusField.clear();
        statusField.appendText("Calling TFTP server...");

        Direction direction =
(directionField.getSelectionModel().getSelectedItem().
            equals("PUT")? Engine.Direction.PUT:
Engine.Direction.GET);

        Mode mode =
            (modeField.getValue().equals("Ascii")?
            Engine.Mode.NETASCII: Engine.Mode.OCTET);

        try {
            Engine tftpEngine = new Engine();
            tftpEngine.addMsgListener(this);
```

```
                    tftpEngine.transfer(
                        InetAddress.getByName(serverIPFi
eld.getText()),

                        direction,
                        mode,
                        fileNameField.getText());
                } catch (UnknownHostException e) {
                statusField.appendText("ERROR Calling
TFTP server.");

                        e.printStackTrace();
                }

            }
        }
```

Once the input fields are validated then we clear the status field and write to the field to say we are starting the call to the server.

Next, we set up two local fields; one of type Direction and the other of type Mode. These are set based on the values held by the choice field in the UI. We access this by calling the getSelectionModel().getSelectionItem() and then calling the equals() method to see if it matches the string value we are looking for. In this way we can find out what value has been selected on the choice field. We then set the enumerator to the required value and in this way, we will ensure we pass the engine a valid value.

We then create a new engine object and make a call to the engine.transfer() method. The method is passed the ip number as an InetAddress, the direction and mode we created earlier and the filename. This is all wrapped in a try/catch clause.

We have now linked our UI to our Engine in the backend, so we are ready to try out our application.

Using your client

So that's all the code we need for our client. What we need to do now is give it a go. For this we will obviously need a TFTP Server.

I suggest using Solarwinds TFTP Server simply because I find it easy to install and use. You can actually use any TFTP compliant server for this so if you have a favourite then please use that.

If you do not have SolarWinds TFTP and wish to use that then go to their web site "https://www.solarwinds.com/free-tools/free-tftp-server". Provide the requested details and download to your machine.

The executable program is provided in a zip file, simply extract the file and run it to install. Accept all the install defaults and then you can launch the application.

Under the 'File' menu option there is the 'Configure' option which presents a dialog box like below

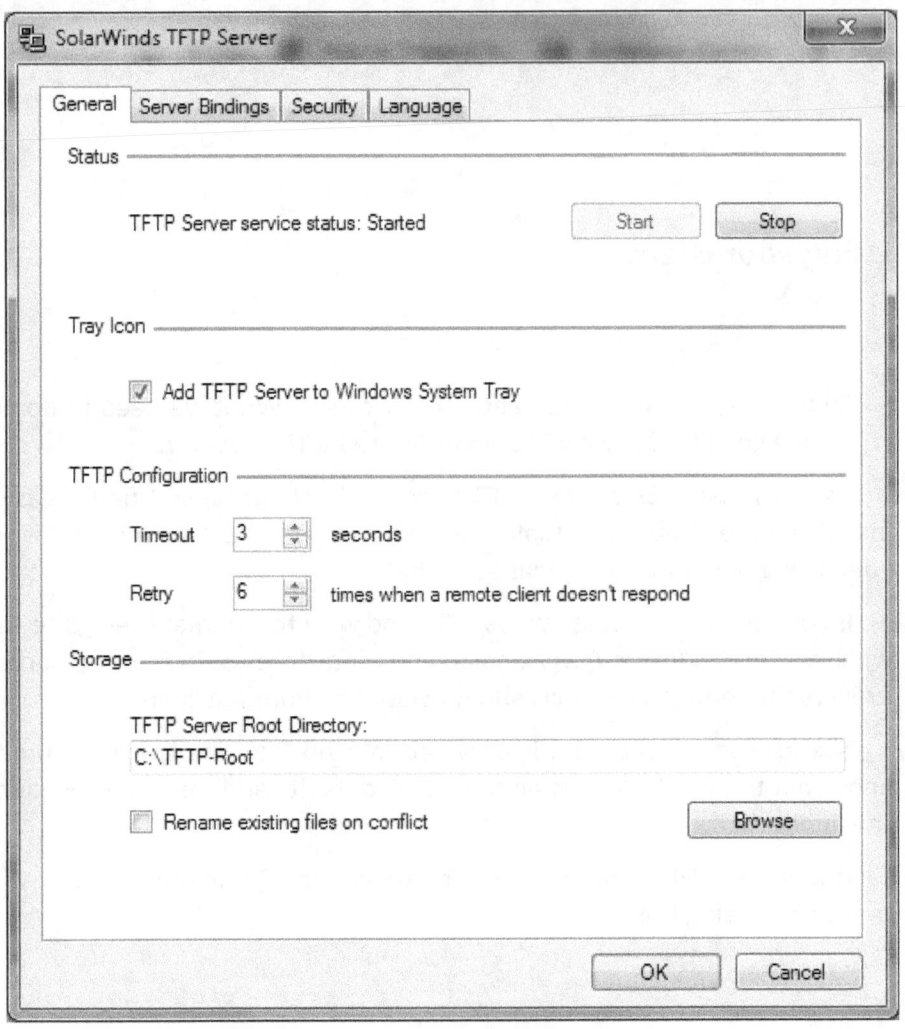

Figure 18 SolarWinds TFTP Server configuration window

Check to see where the server will place files it receives and where it looks for requested files. This is where you need to look to see that your files do indeed turn-up on the server and also what file are available for download.

Now before we can start transferring files between our server and our client, we need to check a few things and put some things in place.

If you are running the server and the client on the same machine, this is fine and is the simplest setup to use. In this case we can use what is known as the IP loopback adapter, this is the IP number that points at itself. This is the number 127.0.0.1, whenever you enter that IP number it sends the IP traffic to itself.

If you have placed the TFTP server on a different machine to the one the client is running on, then you will need to know the IP number for the machine hosting the server. If you are not sure how to do this then on a Windows machine go to the command prompt and type "ipconfig". This will display all the network information for the machine. You may have more than one network address for your machine. Make a note of the IP address you want to use.

Next, if using more than a single machine you need to check that the client machine can see the server. The easiest way to do this is to open a command window on the client machine and then type "ping xxx.xxx.xxx.xxx" where the 'x's are the numbers of the IP number for the server. You should see a reply from the server machine.

```
C:\Users\jmcneil>ping 127.0.0.1

Pinging 127.0.0.1 with 32 bytes of data:
Reply from 127.0.0.1: bytes=32 time<1ms TTL=128
Reply from 127.0.0.1: bytes=32 time<1ms TTL=128
Reply from 127.0.0.1: bytes=32 time<1ms TTL=128
Reply from 127.0.0.1: bytes=32 time<1ms TTL=128

Ping statistics for 127.0.0.1:
    Packets: Sent = 4, Received = 4, Lost = 0 (0% loss),
Approximate round trip times in milli-seconds:
    Minimum = 0ms, Maximum = 0ms, Average = 0ms
```

Figure 19 using ping to check connection to the server

We also need to place some files on our server and client, so we have something to send and receive. Locate some files on your machine or use your favourite text editor to create some files. Place some files in the root directory of the TFTP server.

The rest of the files you can place in the directory the TFTP Client will look in when sending files to the server. The client uses the project root directory for files. This means that the files need to be placed in the project directory of the workspace. In my case it would be:

"C:\Users\jmcneil\Documents\workspace\ClientTFTP"

If we run our ClientTFTP from Eclipse, we will be presented with our interface. The best way to check we are in fact using the correct directories is to make a call to get files from the server. If the call is successful, then the files will turn up in the client directory where we have placed the files to use when sending to the server.

Once you can pull a file down from the server then try sending a file up to the server. Start with binary file transfers first as these are simpler transfers and once these are working move on to ascii transfers.

If you have access to Linux and Macintosh machines as well as Windows, you might like to try moving ascii files between the various systems to see that the information is preserved.

Appendix A – Network Working Group RFC 1350

Network Working Group	K. Sollins
Request For Comments: 1350	MIT
STD: 33	July 1992
Obsoletes: RFC 783	

THE TFTP PROTOCOL (REVISION 2)

Status of this Memo

This RFC specifies an IAB standards track protocol for the Internet community, and requests discussion and suggestions for improvements. Please refer to the current edition of the "IAB Official Protocol Standards" for the standardization state and status of this protocol. Distribution of this memo is unlimited.

Summary

TFTP is a very simple protocol used to transfer files. It is from this that its name comes, Trivial File Transfer Protocol or TFTP. Each nonterminal packet is acknowledged separately. This document describes the protocol and its types of packets. The document also explains the reasons behind some of the design decisions.

Acknowlegements

The protocol was originally designed by Noel Chiappa, and was redesigned by him, Bob Baldwin and Dave Clark, with comments from Steve Szymanski. The current revision of the document includes modifications stemming from discussions with and suggestions from Larry Allen, Noel Chiappa, Dave Clark, Geoff Cooper, Mike Greenwald, Liza Martin, David Reed, Craig Milo Rogers (of USC-ISI), Kathy Yellick, and the author. The acknowledgement and retransmission scheme was inspired by TCP, and the error mechanism was suggested by PARC's EFTP abort message.

The May, 1992 revision to fix the "Sorcerer's Apprentice" protocol bug [4] and other minor document problems was done by Noel Chiappa.

This research was supported by the Advanced Research Projects Agency of the Department of Defense and was monitored by the Office of Naval Research under contract number N00014-75-C-0661.

1. Purpose

TFTP is a simple protocol to transfer files, and therefore was named the Trivial File Transfer Protocol or TFTP. It has been implemented on top of the Internet User Datagram protocol (UDP or Datagram) [2] so it may be used to move files between machines on different networks implementing UDP. (This should not exclude the possibility of implementing TFTP on top of other datagram protocols.) It is designed to be small and easy to implement. Therefore, it lacks most of the features of a regular FTP. The only thing it can do is read and write files (or mail) from/to a remote server. It cannot list directories, and currently has no provisions for user authentication. In common with other Internet protocols, it passes 8 bit bytes of

data.

Three modes of transfer are currently supported:
netascii (This is ascii as defined in "USA Standard Code
for Information Interchange" [1] with the modifications
specified in "Telnet Protocol Specification" [3].) Note
that it is 8 bit ascii. The term "netascii" will be
used throughout this document to mean this particular
version of ascii.); octet (This replaces the "binary"
mode of previous versions of this document.) raw 8 bit
bytes; mail, netascii characters sent to a user rather
than a file. (The mail mode is obsolete and should not
be implemented or used.) Additional modes can be
defined by pairs of cooperating hosts.

Reference [4] (section 4.2) should be consulted for
further valuable directives and suggestions on TFTP.

2. Overview of the Protocol

Any transfer begins with a request to read or write a
file, which also serves to request a connection. If the
server grants the request, the connection is opened and
the file is sent in fixed length blocks of 512 bytes.
Each data packet contains one block of data, and must be
acknowledged by an acknowledgment packet before the next
packet can be sent. A data packet of less than 512
bytes signals termination of a transfer. If a packet
gets lost in the network, the intended recipient will
timeout and may retransmit his last packet (which may be
data or an acknowledgment), thus causing the sender of
the lost packet to retransmit that lost packet. The
sender has to keep just one packet on hand for
retransmission, since the lock step acknowledgment
guarantees that all older packets have been received.
Notice that both machines involved in a transfer are
considered senders and receivers. One sends data and
receives acknowledgments, the other sends
acknowledgments and receives data.

Most errors cause termination of the connection. An
error is signalled by sending an error packet. This

packet is not acknowledged, and not retransmitted (i.e., a TFTP server or user may terminate after sending an error message), so the other end of the connection may not get it. Therefore timeouts are used to detect such a termination when the error packet has been lost. Errors are caused by three types of events: not being able to satisfy the request (e.g., file not found, access violation, or no such user), receiving a packet which cannot be explained by a delay or duplication in the network (e.g., an incorrectly formed packet), and losing access to a necessary resource (e.g., disk full or access denied during a transfer).

TFTP recognizes only one error condition that does not cause termination, the source port of a received packet being incorrect. In this case, an error packet is sent to the originating host.

This protocol is very restrictive, in order to simplify implementation. For example, the fixed length blocks make allocation straight forward, and the lock step acknowledgement provides flow control and eliminates the need to reorder incoming data packets.

3. Relation to other Protocols

As mentioned TFTP is designed to be implemented on top of the Datagram protocol (UDP). Since Datagram is implemented on the Internet protocol, packets will have an Internet header, a Datagram header, and a TFTP header. Additionally, the packets may have a header (LNI, ARPA header, etc.) to allow them through the local transport medium. As shown in Figure 3-1, the order of the contents of a packet will be: local medium header, if used, Internet header, Datagram header, TFTP header, followed by the remainder of the TFTP packet. (This may or may not be data depending on the type of packet as specified in the TFTP header.) TFTP does not specify any of the values in the Internet header. On the other hand, the source and destination port fields of the Datagram header (its format is given in the appendix) are used by TFTP and the length field reflects the size of the TFTP packet. The transfer identifiers (TID's) used by TFTP are passed to the Datagram layer to be used as ports; therefore they must be between 0 and 65,535. The initialization of TID's is discussed in the section on initial connection protocol.

The TFTP header consists of a 2 byte opcode field which indicates the packet's type (e.g., DATA, ERROR, etc.) These opcodes and the formats of the various types of packets are discussed further in the section on TFTP packets.

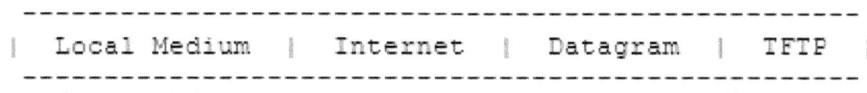

```
---------------------------------------------------
|  Local Medium  |  Internet  |  Datagram  |  TFTP  |
---------------------------------------------------
```

Figure 3-1: Order of Headers

4. Initial Connection Protocol

A transfer is established by sending a request (WRQ to write onto a foreign file system, or RRQ to read from it), and receiving a positive reply, an acknowledgment packet for write, or the first data packet for read. In general an acknowledgment packet will contain the block number of the data packet being acknowledged. Each data packet has associated with it a block number; block numbers are consecutive and begin with one. Since the positive response to a write request is an acknowledgment packet, in this special case the block number will be zero. (Normally, since an acknowledgment packet is acknowledging a data packet, the acknowledgment packet will contain the block number of the data packet being acknowledged.) If the reply is an error packet, then the request has been denied.

In order to create a connection, each end of the connection chooses a TID for itself, to be used for the duration of that connection. The TID's chosen for a connection should be randomly chosen, so that the probability that the same number is chosen twice in immediate succession is very low. Every packet has associated with it the two TID's of the ends of the connection, the source TID and the destination TID. These TID's are handed to the supporting UDP (or other datagram protocol) as the source and destination ports. A requesting host chooses its source TID as described above, and sends its initial request to the known TID 69 decimal (105 octal) on the serving host. The response to the request, under normal operation, uses a TID chosen by the server as its source TID and the TID chosen for the previous message by the requestor as its destination TID. The two chosen TID's are then used for the remainder of the transfer.

As an example, the following shows the steps used to establish a connection to write a file. Note that WRQ, ACK, and DATA are the names of the write request, acknowledgment, and data types of packets respectively. The appendix contains a similar example for reading a file.

1. Host A sends a "WRQ" to host B with source= A's TID, destination= 69.

2. Host B sends a "ACK" (with block number= 0) to host A with source= B's TID, destination= A's TID.

At this point the connection has been established and the first data packet can be sent by Host A with a sequence number of 1. In the next step, and in all succeeding steps, the hosts should make sure that the source TID matches the value that was agreed on in steps 1 and 2. If a source TID does not match, the packet should be discarded as erroneously sent from somewhere else. An error packet should be sent to the source of the incorrect packet, while not disturbing the transfer. This can be done only if the TFTP in fact receives a packet with an incorrect TID. If the supporting

protocols do not allow it, this particular error
condition will not arise.

The following example demonstrates a correct operation
of the protocol in which the above situation can occur.
Host A sends a request to host B. Somewhere in the
network, the request packet is duplicated, and as a
result two acknowledgments are returned to host A, with
different TID's chosen on host B in response to the two
requests.   When the first response arrives, host A
continues the connection. When the second response to
the request arrives, it should be rejected, but there is
no reason to terminate the first connection.   Therefore,
if different TID's are chosen for the two connections on
host B and host A checks the source TID's of the
messages it receives, the first connection can be
maintained while the second is rejected by returning an
error packet.

5. TFTP Packets

TFTP supports five types of packets, all of which have
been mentioned above:

       opcode   operation
          1   Read request (RRQ)
          2   Write request (WRQ)
          3   Data (DATA)
          4   Acknowledgment (ACK)|
          5   Error (ERROR)

The TFTP header of a packet contains the   opcode
associated with that packet.

```
    2 bytes       string     1 byte      string    1 byte
   -----------------------------------------------------
   | Opcode |  Filename  |   0   |    Mode    |   0   |
   -----------------------------------------------------
```

Figure 5-1: RRQ/WRQ packet

RRQ and WRQ packets (opcodes 1 and 2 respectively) have
the format shown in Figure 5-1. The file name is a
sequence of bytes in netascii terminated by a zero byte.
The mode field contains the string "netascii", "octet",
or "mail" (or any combination of upper and lower case,
such as "NETASCII", NetAscii", etc.) in netascii
indicating the three modes defined in the protocol. A
host which receives netascii mode data must translate
the data to its own format. Octet mode is used to
transfer a file that is in the 8-bit format of the
machine from which the file is being transferred. It is
assumed that each type of machine has a single 8-bit
format that is more common, and that that format is
chosen. For example, on a DEC-20, a 36 bit machine,
this is four 8-bit bytes to a word with four bits of
breakage. If a host receives a octet file and then
returns it, the returned file must be identical to the
original. Mail mode uses the name of a mail recipient in
place of a file and must begin with a WRQ. Otherwise it
is identical to netascii mode. The mail recipient string
should be of the form "username" or "username@hostname".
If the second form is used, it allows the option of mail
forwarding by a relay computer.

The discussion above assumes that both the sender and
recipient are operating in the same mode, but there is
no reason that this has to be the case. For example,
one might build a storage server. There is no reason
that such a machine needs to translate netascii into its
own form of text. Rather, the sender might send files
in netascii, but the storage server might simply store
them without translation in 8-bit format. Another such
situation is a problem that currently exists on DEC-20
systems. Neither netascii nor octet accesses all the

bits in a word. One might create a special mode for
such a machine which read all the bits in a word, but in
which the receiver stored the information in 8-bit
format. When such a file is retrieved from the storage
site, it must be restored to its original form to be
useful, so the reverse mode must also be implemented.
The user site will have to remember some information to
achieve this. In both of these examples, the request
packets would specify octet mode to the foreign host,
but the local host would be in some other mode. No such
machine or application specific modes have been
specified in TFTP, but one would be compatible with this
specification.

It is also possible to define other modes for
cooperating pairs of hosts, although this must be done
with care. There is no requirement that any other hosts
implement these. There is no central authority that
will define these modes or assign them names.


```
    2 bytes      2 bytes        n bytes
    ---------------------------------------
   | Opcode  |   Block #  |    Data      |
    ---------------------------------------
```

Figure 5-2: DATA packet

Data is actually transferred in DATA packets depicted in
Figure 5-2. DATA packets (opcode = 3) have a block
number and data field. The block numbers on data
packets begin with one and increase by one for each new
block of data. This restriction allows the program to
use a single number to discriminate between new packets
and duplicates. The data field is from zero to 512 bytes
long. If it is 512 bytes long, the block is not the
last block of data; if it is from zero to 511 bytes
long, it signals the end of the transfer. (See the
section on Normal Termination for details.)

All packets other than duplicate ACK's and those used
for termination are acknowledged unless a timeout occurs

[4]. Sending a DATA packet is an acknowledgment for the first ACK packet of the previous DATA packet. The WRQ and DATA packets are acknowledged by ACK or ERROR packets, while RRQ

```
        2 bytes     2 bytes
        ---------------------
       | Opcode |   Block # |
        ---------------------
```

Figure 5-3: ACK packet

and ACK packets are acknowledged by DATA or ERROR packets. Figure 5-3 depicts an ACK packet; the opcode is 4. The block number in an ACK echoes the block number of the DATA packet being acknowledged. A WRQ is acknowledged with an ACK packet having a block number of zero.

```
   2 bytes      2 bytes        string     1 byte
   -------------------------------------------------
  | Opcode |   ErrorCode |   ErrMsg   |   0  |
   -------------------------------------------------
```

Figure 5-4: ERROR packet

An ERROR packet (opcode 5) takes the form depicted in Figure 5-4. An ERROR packet can be the acknowledgment of any other type of packet. The error code is an integer indicating the nature of the error. A table of values and meanings is given in the appendix. (Note that several error codes have been added to this version of this document.) The error message is intended for human consumption, and should be in netascii. Like all other strings, it is terminated with a zero byte.

6. Normal Termination

The end of a transfer is marked by a DATA packet that contains between 0 and 511 bytes of data (i.e., Datagram length < 516). This packet is acknowledged by an ACK packet like all other DATA packets. The host acknowledging the final DATA packet may terminate its side of the connection on sending the final ACK. On the other hand, dallying is encouraged. This means that the host sending the final ACK will wait for a while before terminating in order to retransmit the final ACK if it has been lost. The acknowledger will know that the ACK has been lost if it receives the final DATA packet again. The host sending the last DATA must retransmit it until the packet is acknowledged or the sending host times out. If the response is an ACK, the transmission was completed successfully. If the sender of the data times out and is not prepared to retransmit any more, the transfer may still have been completed successfully, after which the acknowledger or network may have experienced a problem. It is also possible in this case that the transfer was unsuccessful. In any case, the connection has been closed.

7. Premature Termination

If a request can not be granted, or some error occurs during the transfer, then an ERROR packet (opcode 5) is sent. This is only a courtesy since it will not be retransmitted or acknowledged, so it may never be received. Timeouts must also be used to detect errors.

I. Appendix

Order of Headers

```
                                          2 bytes
     ----------------------------------------------------------
    |  Local Medium  |  Internet  |  Datagram  |  TFTP Opcode  |
     ----------------------------------------------------------
```

TFTP Formats

```
    Type    Op #      Format without header

            2 bytes      string     1 byte      string    1 byte
            -------------------------------------------------------
    RRQ/    | 01/02 |  Filename  |   0   |     Mode     |   0   |
    WRQ     -------------------------------------------------------
            2 bytes     2 bytes           n bytes
            ----------------------------------------
    DATA    | 03     |   Block #  |    Data    |
            ----------------------------------------
            2 bytes     2 bytes
            --------------------
    ACK     | 04     |   Block #  |
            --------------------
            2 bytes   2 bytes           string      1 byte
            ----------------------------------------------
    ERROR | 05      |  ErrorCode  |  ErrMsg  |   0   |
            ----------------------------------------------
```

Initial Connection Protocol for reading a file

1. Host A sends a "RRQ" to host B with source= A's TID, destination= 69.

2. Host B sends a "DATA" (with block number= 1) to host A with source= B's TID, destination= A's TID.

Error Codes

    Value   Meaning

    0   Not defined, see error message (if any).
    1   File not found.
    2   Access violation.
    3   Disk full or allocation exceeded.
    4   Illegal TFTP operation.
    5   Unknown transfer ID.
    6   File already exists.
    7   No such user.

Internet User Datagram Header [2]

(This has been included only for convenience. TFTP need not be implemented on top of the Internet User Datagram Protocol.)

    Format

```
0                   1                   2                   3
0 1 2 3 4 5 6 7 8 9 0 1 2 3 4 5 6 7 8 9 0 1 2 3 4 5 6 7 8 9 0 1
+-+-+-+-+-+-+-+-+-+-+-+-+-+-+-+-+-+-+-+-+-+-+-+-+-+-+-+-+-+-+-+-+
|          Source Port          |       Destination Port        |
+-+-+-+-+-+-+-+-+-+-+-+-+-+-+-+-+-+-+-+-+-+-+-+-+-+-+-+-+-+-+-+-+
|            Length             |           Checksum            |
+-+-+-+-+-+-+-+-+-+-+-+-+-+-+-+-+-+-+-+-+-+-+-+-+-+-+-+-+-+-+-+-+
```

Values of Fields

Source Port - Picked by originator of packet.

Dest. Port - Picked by destination machine (69 for RRQ or WRQ).

Length - Number of bytes in UDP packet, including UDP header.

Checksum - Reference 2 describes rules for computing checksum. (The implementor of this should be sure that the correct algorithm is used here.) field contains zero if unused.

Note: TFTP passes transfer identifiers (TID's) to the Internet User Datagram protocol to be used as the source and destination ports.

References

[1]   USA Standard Code for Information Interchange, USASI X3.4-1968.

[2]   Postel, J., "User Datagram Protocol," RFC 768, USC/Information Sciences Institute, 28 August 1980.

[3]   Postel, J., "Telnet Protocol Specification," RFC 764, USC/Information Sciences Institute, June, 1980.

[4]   Braden, R., Editor, "Requirements for Internet Hosts -- Application and Support", RFC 1123, USC/Information Sciences Institute, October 1989.

Security Considerations

Since TFTP includes no login or access control mechanisms, care must be taken in the rights granted to a TFTP server process so as not to violate the security of the server hosts file system. TFTP is often installed with controls such that only files that have public read access are available via TFTP and writing files via TFTP is disallowed.

Author's Address

Karen R. Sollins

Massachusetts Institute of Technology

Laboratory for Computer Science

545 Technology Square

Cambridge, MA 02139-1986

Phone: (617) 253-6006

EMail: SOLLINS@LCS.MIT.EDU

Appendix B - Installing Java

For all the code covered here we will be using Java standard edition. In order to develop our Java application, we will need to install Java Development Kit (JDK) version 8 or greater.

You need to be aware that in 2018 Oracle, who control Java, made a change to the way in which the product is licensed. The JDK offered by Oracle restricts how the product can be freely used. Instead there is now a JDK offered under the GNU General Public License, version 2 agreement which makes greater provision for free use. If you are using a Java version greater than version 8 then please be aware of these two differences.

To start with let us download the Java JDK and install this. I would suggest getting the latest version of Java if you do not already have Java installed. If you have Java JDK version 8 or above, then you can just use the version you have.

To download Java, go to https://jdk.java.net/. From there follow the link to the latest version of the JDK. This takes you to a page where Java is offered for the various supported platforms. You should be able to find versions for Linux, MacOS and Windows. Click on the link download. The download is usually provided as a compressed file and to install unpack the file to your hard drive.

Appendix C - Installing Scene Builder

Scene Builder is provided by Gluon https://gluonhq.com/products/scene-builder/. The download is provided as an installer so once downloaded just run the download file and it will install to your machine. To launch Scene Builder, you can launch it from the start menu.

Appendix D - Installing Eclipse

All the code for the application is developed using an Integrated Development Environment (IDE). There are many products in the market place such as NetBeans, IntelliJ and Eclipse and they usually offer a free version for none commercial development.

For all the code covered here we will be using Eclipse as the IDE. Eclipse is run by the Eclipse Foundation and can be found at their website https://www.eclipse.org/.

Go to the web site and look for the download link. You are looking for the Eclipse for Java IDE download link. Usually the site will detect the operating system you are using and the architecture in use and offer you the download link for your machine. If you are planning to install to a different machine, then make sure you select the link that offers alternative packages, so you can select the version you require. You will need Eclipse version 4.4 or later but as 4.4 is quite dated now so this should not be an issue.

The download comes in the form of a compressed file and once again unpack this to your hard drive.

To start Eclipse, go to the directory where Eclipse was installed and locate the file "eclipse.exe" and run this. This will start Eclipse and the first time the application starts you will be asked to specify a location for the workspace. The workspace is simply a location where all the java projects will be placed along with all the files associated with the project. You can select anywhere you want to place the workspace, but I would suggest you pick somewhere to can easily find.

Now that Eclipse is up and running, we need to install the JavaFX component. The easiest way to do this is to use the Eclipse "Install New

Software" option found under the Help menu option. This opens a dialog box

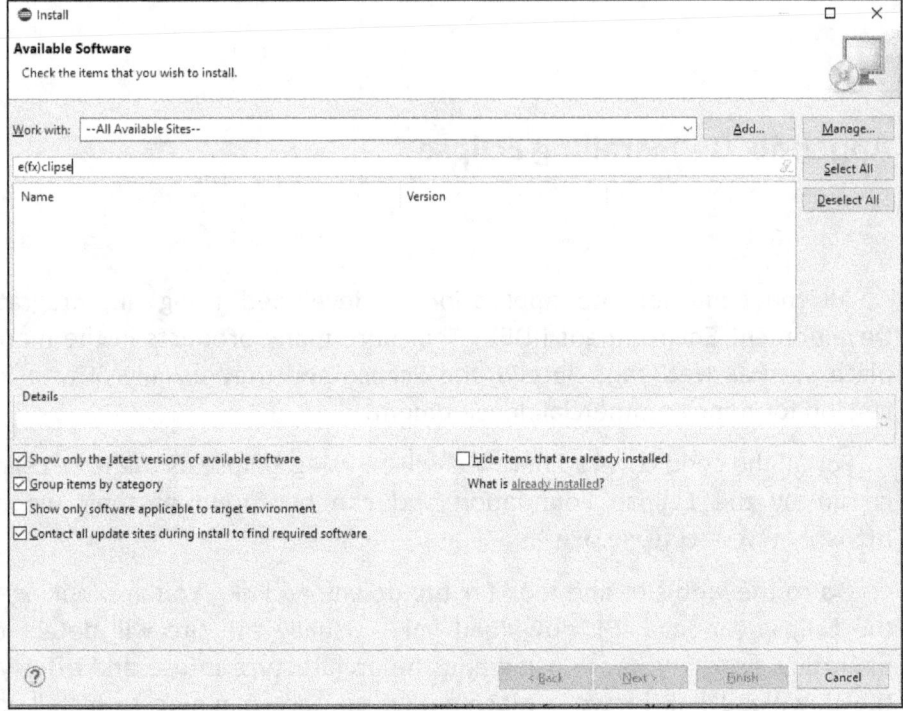

Figure 20 install new software window

Select work with all available sites. This options is slower but ensures you get a match for your search term. Then below the "work with" drop down option enter "e(fx)clispe" in the search field and press the "Select All" button.

Below will appear a list of options that the search has found. One of these will be "e(fx)clipse" and if you expand this option you will see a list of FX components.

∨ e(fx)clipse - IDE	3.0.0.201705220750	org.eclipse.fx.ide.feature.fe
> e(fx)clipse - IDE - Basic	3.0.0.201705220750	org.eclipse.fx.ide.basic.feat
e(fx)clipse - IDE - Converter	3.0.0.201705220750	org.eclipse.fx.ide.converter
> e(fx)clipse - IDE - CSS	3.0.0.201705220750	org.eclipse.fx.ide.css.featur
e(fx)clipse - IDE - DSL to setup JavaFX based code editors	3.0.0.201705220750	org.eclipse.fx.ide.ldef.featu
> e(fx)clipse - IDE - FXGraph	3.0.0.201705220750	org.eclipse.fx.ide.fxgraph.f
> e(fx)clipse - IDE - FXML	3.0.0.201705220750	org.eclipse.fx.ide.fxml.featu
e(fx)clipse - IDE - GModel Feature	3.0.0.201705220750	org.eclipse.fx.ide.gmod.fea
e(fx)clipse - IDE - I10n support	3.0.0.201705220750	org.eclipse.fx.ide.I10n.featu
> e(fx)clipse - IDE - PDE	3.0.0.201705220750	org.eclipse.fx.ide.pde.featu
> e(fx)clipse - IDE - RRobot	3.0.0.201705220750	org.eclipse.fx.ide.rrobot.fea

Figure 21 e(fx)clipse IDE plugin

Select the "e(fx)clipse – IDE" option and press the "Finish" button to install the option.

With the JavaFX module now installed we just need to configure Eclipse to use it and also use SceneBuilder.

We need to ensure that we always use the correct version of Java when building our project. It is possible to have several versions of Java installed on the same machine, so it makes sense to set this up. Go to "Eclipse Preferences" which can be found under the "Windows" menu option. Navigate to the Java Installed JREs (Java Runtime Environnments). Add the Java version installed earlier and remove any other versions. This ensures the Java version we have installed is the default Java version that Eclipse will use.

Staying in the preferences area we now need to go to the Java Compiler section and set the Java Compliance level to 1.8 or later.

Still within the preferences section we need to go to the JavaFX section and set the location of the SceneBuilder executable file.

This done we have installed Eclipse, installed JavaFX and configured Eclipse to use our build tools.